What Everyone
Should Know About

the
Afterlife

A Biblical View of
What Lies Beyond the Grave

Rob Phillips

Contents

Introduction

You're going to live forever. Really. From the moment God began forming you in your mother's womb, He designed you as an everlasting person, which means that physical death is not the end of your existence. In fact, even when you draw your last breath, your life continues, unbroken, into eternity.

Not everyone believes this, of course. Those who hold to a naturalistic worldview argue that physical death spells the end of your existence — forever; if you live on, it is only in the memory of others or through the residual impact of your life. Others believe your soul sleeps, or ceases to exist, at physical death, awaiting a future resurrection in which a "second chance" determines whether you'll live forever or be annihilated. Still others look to karma to set things right through reincarnation or rebirth.

No doubt, these views — and their countless shades of variance — cannot all be true. But are *any* of them reliable? What really happens to us at death? Can we know, on this side of the grave, what lies beyond? The Bible answers with a resounding yes!

The pages that follow briefly address what God reveals to us in Scripture about the afterlife. I encourage you to read these short chapters, consider the study questions associated with each topic, and grasp this marvelous truth: An infinite and holy Creator cares so much about you that He sacrificed His Son to secure everlasting life for you.

While all people share a common dignity as beings created in God's image, we do not necessarily share a common destiny. We all pass through the portal of death, but what lies beyond is everlasting existence either in the presence of our Creator or, by our own choice, in isolation from Him. Our response to God's offer of salvation carries everlasting consequences.

Read on and see what every person should know about what lies beyond the grave.

Rob Phillips

July 1, 2017

one
Ten Biblical Truths About the Afterlife

Three-year-old Colton Burpo had a near-death experience (NDE) while on the operating table. When it was over, he described his "three minutes in heaven" in vivid detail, including encounters with Samson, John the Baptist, and Jesus, who had sea-blue eyes and owned a rainbow-colored horse.

Colton's father, a Wesleyan pastor, believes the lad's experience was real because Colton shared it with "the simple conviction of an eyewitness."[1]

You may read Colton's story in *Heaven is for Real: A Little Boy's Astounding Story of His Trip to Heaven and Back*,[2] which ruled the best-seller list for 44 weeks. Millions of people have devoured the book, watched the youngster's appearances on TV shows, and viewed the major motion picture based on his story.

Less popular, but equally intriguing, are books about NDEs in which people "die" for brief periods and experience the horrors of hell. *To Hell and Back* by cardiologist Maurice Rollins, for example, tells us that hellish NDEs have to be recorded and verified immediately after the person "returns," or the horrifying memories are repressed.[3]

In any case, stories like Colton's appeal to our desire to know more about the afterlife.

Sincerely wrong

I have never met Colton or his father. And I have no reason to doubt that Colton had an experience of some kind, or that his father is sincere in sharing what his son observed. What concerns me is something Christian apologist Hank Hanegraaff articulated when he wrote that "our culture has forgotten one very simple fact: you can be sincere and still be wrong."[4]

It is important for Christians to realize that any reports of the afterlife must be measured against Scripture. God has chosen not to answer every question about life after death in His Word, but He gives us enough information to know at least 10 biblical truths:

1. Death is not the end of life. In perhaps the earliest biblical reference to resurrection, Job expresses confidence that in his flesh he will see God (Job 19:26). After his death, Samuel appears to Saul (1 Samuel 28), and Moses and Elijah appear with Jesus on the Mount of Transfiguration (Matt. 17:1-4). Jesus tells the story of Lazarus and the rich man to describe life beyond the grave (Luke 16:19-31). And the apostles Paul and John are given glimpses into heaven (2 Cor. 12:1-4; Revelation 1-22).

2. There is conscious existence beyond the grave. Jesus' story of Lazarus and the rich man offers graphic details of the afterlife, showing us that people continue to think, remember, experience pain, communicate, and understand where they are — and why (Luke 16:19-31).

3. We maintain our identities. King Saul recognizes Samuel after the witch of Endor summons him from the dead (or, more properly, the Lord beckons him - 1 Samuel 28). Peter, James, and John identify Moses and Elijah on the Mount of Transfiguration even though they have never met (Matt. 17:1-4). The rich man in Jesus' parable sees both Lazarus and Abraham across the great divide in *Hades* (Luke 16:19-31).

4. We have memories of life on earth. The rich man remembers that he has five brothers, and he asks Abraham to send Lazarus back to earth to warn them of torment. Apparently, the rich man realizes he is not permitted to be set free.

5. We await future resurrection. Jesus tells us all who are in the graves will hear His voice one day and "come out" (John 5:28-29). Paul writes that Christians will receive glorified bodies (1 Corinthians 15), while John sees unbelievers receiving resurrected bodies prepared for eternal separation from God (Rev. 20:11-15).

6. We await final judgment. Christians will stand before the judgment seat of Christ (2 Cor. 5:10). Unbelievers will stand in judgment before the great white throne (Rev. 20:11-15).

7. Believers are destined for life with Christ in the new heavens and new earth. The apostle John describes what it will be like when Jesus renovates our sinful and fallen world (Revelation 21-22).

8. Unbelievers are destined for hell and everlasting separation from God. "Outer darkness" awaits those who reject Christ. Not that God is cruel. Unbelievers choose eternity on their own terms. As C.S. Lewis writes in *The Problem of Pain*, "I willingly believe that the damned are, in one sense, successful, rebels to the end; that the gates of hell are locked on the inside."[5]

9. Our choices *now* have everlasting consequences. Jesus asks the question every person must answer: "Who do you say that I am?" (Matt. 16:15). And we must answer in this life, for there are no second chances beyond the grave (Heb. 9:27).

10. God has chosen not to reveal everything about the afterlife at this time. Paul is prevented from sharing his experiences in "paradise" (2 Cor. 12:4). John is forbidden from revealing everything he hears in the Apocalypse (Rev. 10:4). For now, we should be content with what God has revealed in Scripture.

Think

Questions for personal or group study

Why do you think so many stories of near-death experiences are at odds with Scripture?

How does our understanding of the afterlife progress as we move from the Old Testament to the New Testament? Why is it important to understand the concept of "progressive revelation" — God's increased revelation of Himself and His will over time in Scripture?

What are some popular but unbiblical beliefs about life after death?

Why do you think final judgment for all people comes after their resurrection and not immediately after death?

Do you think the depictions of fiery judgment in Scripture should be taken literally? Why or why not?

Share

Talking points for discussing life after death

- Any reports of the afterlife must be measured against Scripture. God has chosen not to answer every question about life after death in His Word, but He gives us enough information to know many profound truths.

- The Bible is clear that death is not the end of life; people retain conscious existence beyond the grave.

- We also keep our identities after death and apparently have at least some memories of our lives on earth.

- At death, our souls / spirits separate from our bodies, and we await resurrection and final judgment.

- Those who have trusted in Christ are destined to enjoy eternity with Him in the new heavens and new earth. People who reject Christ have chosen to spend eternity apart from Him in hell.

- Our choices now — on this side of the grave — have everlasting consequences.

two
Sheol and the Afterlife

While the doctrines pertaining to life beyond the grave are not fully developed in the Old Testament, there is ample evidence in the Hebrew Scriptures that the souls of people survive death. A key term used to describe the intermediate destiny of the deceased is *Sheol*.

Old Testament writers use the Hebrew word *Sheol* 65 times to describe the abode of the dead. It communicates the reality of human mortality and the impact of one's life on his or her destiny.

Ancient Israelites believed in life beyond the grave, borne out in such passages as Isa. 14:9-15, where *Sheol* contains "the spirits of the departed," and 1 Sam. 28:13, where the deceased prophet Samuel temporarily appears as "a spirit form coming up out of the earth."

It's important to note that while the Old Testament consistently refers to the body as going to the grave, it always refers to the soul or spirit of people as going to *Sheol*, according to Robert A. Morey in *Death and the Afterlife*.

One source of confusion is the manner in which the King James Version translates *Sheol*, according to Morey: "The KJV translates Sheol as 'hell' 31 times, 'grave' 31 times, and 'pit' three times. Because of this inconsistency of translation, such groups as the Adventists ... and Jehovah's Witnesses have taught that Sheol means the grave."[1]

Fortunately, he adds, lexicons and rabbinic literature consistently understand *Sheol* as the place where the souls or spirits of persons go at death.

Down to *Sheol*

In fact, the first occurrence of *Sheol* in the Old Testament (Gen. 37:35) cannot possibly mean "grave." As Jacob holds the bloodied remnants of Joseph's coat, he laments about his deceased boy, "I will go down to *Sheol* to my son, mourning."

Whatever else *Sheol* may mean, in this passage it cannot mean Joseph's grave, for Jacob believes his son has been devoured by wild animals and thus has no grave. Jacob could not be buried in a common grave with Joseph.

According to the context, Jacob anticipates being reunited with Joseph in the underworld. He speaks of going "down" because it is assumed that *Sheol* is the place of departed spirits, likely a hollow place in the center of the earth.

There are other factors about *Sheol* to consider, among them:

1. When Old Testament writers want to identify the grave, they often use the Hebrew word *Kever*, which is contrasted with *Sheol*. *Kever* is the fate of the body, while *Sheol* is the fate of the soul.

2. In the Septuagint, the Greek translation of the Old Testament, *Sheol* is never translated as *mneema*, the Greek word for grave.

3. *Sheol* is "under the earth" or "the underworld," while graves in Old Testament times tend to be built as sepulchers above the earth, in caves, or in holes in the earth.

4. While bodies are unconscious in the grave, those in *Sheol* are viewed as conscious.

Progressive revelation

God's revelation in Scripture is progressive, meaning that as we move through the Bible, God reveals additional truths that build upon the others. With this in mind, we see the concept of *Sheol* develop throughout the Old Testament. While it is described as dark (Lam. 3:6), and a place of helplessness (Ps. 88:4), trouble, and sorrow (Ps. 116:3), God is both present in *Sheol* (Ps. 139:8) and able to deliver from it (Ps. 16:10; 49:15).

This leads some commentators to argue that there are two compartments in *Sheol*, one for the wicked and another for the righteous. Later Jewish literature describes these divisions, in which people experience a foretaste of their final destiny (see Enoch 22:1-14, an ancient Jewish work not part of the biblical canon).

Jesus' story of Lazarus and the rich man seems to expand on this depiction, applying the Greek word *Hades* to the realm of the dead (Luke 16:19-31).

Other scholars contend, however, that *Sheol* is only for the wicked, because God rescues the spirits of the righteous from *Sheol* and takes them to a place of blessedness.

The ascension of Enoch and Elijah to heaven, for example, is cited to support the belief that the righteous under the old covenant could be taken directly into God's presence at the end of their earthly lives.

Today, we know that the souls/spirits of Christians enter heaven immediately upon death (2 Cor. 5:6-8). Evidently, the souls of unbelievers remain in *Sheol* where they await resurrection and final judgment.

Think

Questions for personal or group study

In what ways are *Sheol* and the grave different?

How might you respond to the person who argues that the Old Testament says nothing about life after death?

Why is it not possible for *Sheol* to mean a burial place?

Why do you think the Holy Spirit gives us such a limited view of life after death in the Scriptures — leaving us with so many unanswered questions?

What are the dangers of seeking to communicate with the deceased?

Share

Talking points for discussing *Sheol* and the afterlife

- While the doctrines pertaining to life beyond the grave are not fully developed in the Old Testament, there is ample evidence in the Hebrew Scriptures that the souls of people survive death.

- Old Testament writers use the Hebrew word *Sheol* 65 times to describe the abode of the dead.

- While the Old Testament consistently refers to the body as going to the grave, it always refers to the soul or spirit of a person as going to *Sheol*.

- Some Bible commentators contend that there are two compartments in *Sheol*, one for the wicked and another for the righteous.

- Other scholars say that *Sheol* is only for the wicked, while God rescues the spirits of the righteous from *Sheol* and takes them to a place of blessedness.

- In either case, the Old Testament testifies to the reality of life beyond the grave.

three
Hades and the Afterlife

Hades is a Greek god whose name means "The Unseen." He is depicted as lord of the underworld, or the abode of the dead. So, it should come as no surprise that Jesus and the New Testament writers borrow from the familiar term *Hades* to describe the realm of departed spirits. What's more, they cut through the mythology to present a more accurate picture of the afterlife.

The word *Hades* appears 10 times in the New Testament, forming a linguistic bridge that takes us from the Old Testament view of life beyond the grave (in *Sheol*) to the

New Testament position. In coming to a biblically faithful understanding of *Hades*, it's important to state what the word does *not* mean.

It does not mean death, because the Greek word *thanatos* is used for death in the New Testament. Further, death (*thanatos*) and *Hades* appear together in Rev. 1:18, so they cannot mean the same thing.

Second, it cannot mean grave, because the Greek work *mneema* depicts the place where the bodies of the deceased are buried.

Third, it cannot mean hell, the place of final punishment for the wicked, because the Greek word *Gehenna* is used for hell in the New Testament, along with other terms like "outer darkness," "eternal fire," and "lake of fire." Further, *Hades* is cast into the lake of fire in Rev. 20:14.

Fourth, *Hades* is not heaven, which is the intermediate state of Christian souls between death and resurrection, because the Greek word *ouranos* depicts heaven.

Progressive revelation

While *Hades* is consistently used in the Septuagint as the Greek equivalent of the Hebrew term *Sheol*, this does not mean *Hades* should be limited to the Old Testament understanding of the afterlife.

As we move through the Bible, God reveals more truths so that His revelation in Scripture may be described as progressive. Put another way, the New Testament picks up where the Old Testament leaves off by further developing our understanding of what happens to the soul after death.

During the period between the Old and New Testaments, the Jewish concept of *Sheol* progressed to the point where it was believed that *Sheol* had two distinct compartments: torment, and Abraham's bosom or paradise.

This rabbinic understanding of *Sheol* is the basis for Jesus' story of Lazarus and the rich man, in which Jesus uses the Greek word *Hades* (Luke 16:19-31). The rich man dies and finds himself in torment in *Hades*. Angels, on the other hand, carry Lazarus to Abraham's bosom, presumably the other compartment of *Hades*.

The conversation between Abraham and the rich man, the description of the rich man's consciousness and suffering, and the impassable gulf between the two compartments provide further details about *Hades* that build on the Old Testament understanding of life beyond the grave.

Context and Hades

Nevertheless, we should acknowledge that *Hades* is a somewhat flexible term whose precise meaning depends on context. Consider:

In Matt. 11:23-24 and Luke 10:15, Jesus uses *Hades* to depict the destruction of Capernaum.

In Matt. 16:18, Jesus assures His followers that the shadowy afterlife (*Hades*) cannot overpower His church because He has come to conquer sin and death.

In Luke 16:19-31, Jesus describes the torment suffered by the rich man in *Hades*, where a great chasm separates the rich man from Lazarus and Abraham.

In Acts 2:25-31, Peter quotes from Psalm 16:8-11 to make it clear that Jesus, unlike David, did not remain among the dead in *Hades* but rose from the dead without His flesh suffering corruption.

In Rev. 1:18, Jesus holds the keys of death and *Hades*, meaning He has authority over death and its consequences.

Finally, in Rev. 20:13-14, Death and *Hades* are personified as giving up their dead. Then, Death and *Hades* are thrown into the lake of fire. There is no more physical death, and no more temporary abode for the wicked dead in *Hades*.

Absent from the body

Some New Testament commentators believe Jesus escorted the Old Testament saints from *Hades* into heaven during the days between His death and resurrection, citing Eph. 4:8-9 and 1 Peter 3:18-22. Others dispute this, arguing that saints under the old covenant entered heaven immediately after death.

In any case, the New Testament describes believers who die *after* Christ's resurrection as entering heaven directly upon death (Phil. 1:23). There, they are present with the Lord (2 Cor. 5:6-8), worshiping with the angelic hosts of heaven and other redeemed people at the altar of God (Heb. 12:22-23; Rev. 6:9-11).

Meanwhile, the souls of deceased unbelievers continue to populate *Hades*, awaiting resurrection and final judgment, at which time they stand before the great white throne and are cast into *Gehenna*, which is the focus of the next chapter.

Think

How are *Hades* and *Sheol* similar?

Why is *Hades* not the same as hell?

What does Jesus reveal about *Hades* in the parable of Lazarus and the rich man (Luke 16:19-31)? And what are the potential dangers of taking every detail literally?

Read Eph. 4:8-9 and 1 Peter 3:18-22. Do you think these passages support the belief that Jesus escorted Old Testament saints to heaven during the time between His death and resurrection? What are some other possible interpretations of these verses?

Where do followers of Jesus go immediately upon death? Where do unbelievers go today when they die?

Share

Talking points for discussing *Hades* and the afterlife

- The word *Hades* appears 10 times in the New Testament, forming a linguistic bridge that takes us from the Old Testament view of life beyond the grave (in *Sheol*) to the New Testament position.

- *Hades* is the abode of the dead, similar to *Sheol* in the Old Testament.

- *Hades* is not death, the grave, hell, or heaven; the New Testament uses different Greek words to describe these realities.

- The New Testament picks up where the Old Testament leaves off by further developing our understanding of what happens to the soul after death.

- *Hades,* along with Death, is destined for the lake of fire. There will be no more physical death, and no more temporary abode for the wicked dead.

four
Does the Bible Teach Purgatory?

Do some Christians undergo purification from the stain of sin for a time between death and entrance into heaven? Many who answer yes to that question embrace the doctrine of purgatory, which became official Roman Catholic dogma in A.D. 1438.

Simply stated, purgatory is a place or state of suffering where the dead bound for heaven achieve the holiness necessary to enter into the presence of God. It should be noted, according to Catholic teaching, that some saints go directly to heaven upon death, needing no purification, while those who die in the state of unrepented mortal sin find themselves at once, and eternally, in hell. All those in purgatory ultimately make it to heaven.

As the *Catechism of the Catholic Church* explains, "All who die in God's grace and friendship, but still imperfectly purified, are indeed assured of their eternal salvation; but after death they undergo purification, so as to achieve the holiness necessary to enter the joy of heaven."[1]

The *Pocket Catholic Dictionary* puts it this way: "The souls of those who have died in the state of grace suffer for a time in purging that prepares them to enter heaven. The purpose of purgatory is to cleanse one of imperfections, venial sins, and faults, and to remit or do away with the temporal punishment due to mortal sins that have been forgiven in the Sacrament of Penance. It is an intermediate state in which the departed souls can atone for unforgiven sins before receiving their final reward."[2]

The amount of time one spends in purgatory depends on the degree of purging needed. "Pope Gregory I taught that baptism absolves us of original sin but that we have to remit payment for our actual sins," according to Chad Owen Brand. "This purging is a preparation of the soul for heaven."[3]

Some proponents of purgatory, however, argue that because the afterlife is experienced outside the element of time, purgatory should be seen as a state or dimension rather than as a place. Indeed, Catholic theologians speak of the great diversity of purgatorial suffering in both its intensity and its duration.[4]

Even so, the question for evangelical Christians is: Does the Bible support the doctrine of purgatory?

An escape through fire

Catholic apologists cite both the Apocrypha (a collection of writings found in the Catholic Bible but excluded from the 66 books of the Protestant canon) and the New Testament to support their belief in purgatory.

For example, the words of Jesus in Matt. 12:32 are cited to support the idea that sins may be forgiven in the age to come. But Jesus is not speaking of post-mortem suffering to atone for one's own sins; He is pointing out that there is no forgiveness available — ever — to the one who blasphemes the Holy Spirit.

Another oft-quoted passage is Matt. 5:25-26, where Jesus warns His followers to reach settlements quickly with adversaries lest they be thrown into prison until they pay the last penny. By extension, it is argued that souls with a sin debt must remit payment beyond the grave before entering heaven. But our Lord is not speaking about an after-death prison; He is providing practical advice for living peaceably among our neighbors in the here and now.

The most-often cited New Testament passage in favor of purgatory is 1 Cor. 3:10-15, in which Paul describes the judgment of believers' works. Verse 15 reads, "If anyone's work is burned up, it will be lost, but he will be saved; yet it will be like an escape through fire."

Even a cursory reading of this passage shows that Paul is speaking of believers' *works* being judged by fire, not of their *sins* being purged through temporal punishment. In verse 14, Paul makes it clear that Christ's judgment of our works results in a reward, or a wage.

Believers' works, not their sins, are purged at the judgment seat of Christ. Paul uses figurative language to tell us the fire "discloses" or "tests" the quality of a Christian's works. Other New Testament passages speak of a time after resurrection when we give an account of our Christian stewardship, resulting in rewards or loss of rewards (see Rom. 14:10-12 and 2 Cor. 5:10).

Christ's sufficiency

Perhaps the strongest argument against the doctrine of purgatory is that it undermines the sufficiency of Christ. Just before His death on the cross, Jesus declares triumphantly, "It is finished!" (John 19:30). Among other things, this means the work of redemption is complete and that no more sacrifice for sins is required. The wrath of God has been satisfied as the One who knew no sin became sin for us, so that we might become the righteousness of God in Christ (2 Cor. 5:21).

The writer of Hebrews echoes this truth: "After making purification for sins, He [Jesus] sat down at the right hand of the Majesty on high" (1:3b). Further, "For by one offering He has perfected forever those who are sanctified" (10:14).

Jesus paid our sin debt in full on the cross. There is nothing we can do to be forgiven of sins except to believe on the Lord Jesus Christ, at which time the penalty for sins — past, present, and future — is removed. We have passed from spiritual death into spiritual life and no longer face condemnation (John 5:24; Rom. 8:1).

Believers are declared in right standing with God (justified) and granted everlasting life. Then, through the lifelong process of sanctification, the indwelling Holy Spirit conforms believers to the image of Christ, completing the process in glorification, which occurs at the resurrection of the just.

Sins committed after justification affect our fellowship with Christ and should be confessed, but justification is never revoked, and the purging of sins never falls on our shoulders. We may suffer *because* of our sins, but only Jesus suffered *for* our sins.

Treasury of merit

Another danger in the doctrine of purgatory is the idea of indulgences, which are believed to partially or fully cancel the debt of temporal punishment in purgatory. Once earned, these withdrawals from the Catholic Church's "treasury of merit," earned by the works and prayers of Jesus, Mary, and the saints of all ages, may be applied personally or applied to a deceased person believed now to be in purgatory.

Historically, this belief resulted in corrupt practices that spurred Martin Luther to post his 95 Theses to the door of All Saints' Church at Wittenberg, Germany, sparking the Reformation. The head of the Catholic Church in 1517, Pope Leo X, offered indulgences to finance the new St. Peter's Church in Rome. The proclamation by church officials — "as soon as the coin in the coffer rings, the soul from purgatory springs" — set Luther ablaze.[5]

Even so, the Catholic Church's first "pope" (Peter) would have eschewed the very ideas of purgatory and indulgences. Peter writes that the gift of the new birth, through the resurrection of Jesus from the dead, gives us an "inheritance that is imperishable, uncorrupted, and unfading, kept in heaven for you. You are being protected by God's power through faith for a salvation that is ready to be revealed in the last time" (1 Peter 1:4-5).

He goes on to write of Jesus, "He Himself bore our sins in His body on the tree, so that, having died to sins, we might live for righteousness; you have been healed by His wounds" (1 Peter 2:24).

Heaven can't wait

The Bible describes heaven, not purgatory followed by heaven, as the intermediate state between death and resurrection for the follower of Jesus. In 2 Corinthians 5, the apostle Paul describes two different states of existence for the believer. While we are here on earth in our bodies, we are absent from the Lord. And when we are "out of the body" we are "at home with the Lord" (5:8).

If there is an interim step between death and heaven, the Bible makes no mention of it, and we would do well to rest in the plainly stated promises of God's Word. For those who die in the Lord, heaven can't wait, nor should it.

One final thought: While evangelicals may disagree with our Catholic friends over the doctrine of purgatory, we share a common expectation of the return of the Lord, resurrection and final judgment, and new heavens and a new earth.

As the *Catechism of the Catholic Church* declares, "At the end of time, the Kingdom of God will come in its fullness. After the universal judgment, the righteous will reign forever with Christ, glorified in body and soul. The universe itself will be renewed."[6]

Think

Questions for personal or group study

What is the connection between purgatory and indulgences?

Why should we be skeptical of doctrines drawn largely from Apocryphal writings?

While Catholics and evangelicals disagree about purgatory, what beliefs about the afterlife do we hold in common?

What does the doctrine of purgatory say about the sufficiency of Christ's sacrificial and substitutionary death?

What is the difference between purgatory and the judgment seat of Christ?

Share

Talking points for discussing purgatory

- In Catholic teaching, purgatory is a place or state of suffering where the dead bound for heaven achieve the holiness necessary to enter into the presence of God.

- While proponents of purgatory cite several New Testament passages in support of this doctrine, these Scriptures in fact say nothing about an interim state between death and heaven for the righteous. Christians enter immediately into the presence of the Lord upon death.

- Believers' *works*, not their *sins*, are the focus of the judgment seat of Christ.

- Perhaps the strongest argument against the doctrine of purgatory is that it denies the sufficiency of Christ.

- We may suffer *because* of our sins, but only Jesus suffered *for* our sins.

five
Your Future Resurrection

If physical death is not the end of our existence, what happens to our bodies? Why does the Bible speak of future resurrection? And if the immaterial part of us — our souls / spirits — separate from our bodies at death and reside either in a state of blessedness with the Lord (2 Cor. 5:8; Phil. 1:23) or apart from Him in torment (Luke 16:19-31), what need is there for resurrection?

First of all, it's important to note that God created Adam and Eve to live forever in their bodies, and that is His creative intent for us as well. But sin ruins everything. It affects our ability to relate to a holy God. It corrupts our minds, emotions, and wills. It brings a curse on the material universe. And it results in spiritual and physical death.

As a consequence of Adam's sin, all people experience pain, suffering, injury, aging, and death. Nature itself is in the throes of a struggle with entropy. So, if Jesus paid our sin debt in full, it means He not only restores believers to a right relationship with Him; He also reverses the effects of the Fall, including physical death and a cursed environment.

In other words, the Christian's salvation is completed in what the apostle Paul calls "glorification," the resurrection and perfection of our bodies, which are made like the risen body of Jesus. This final chapter in redemption is so certain that Paul refers to it in the past tense, along with God's foreknowledge, predestination, calling, and justification (Rom. 8:29-30). Followers of Jesus ultimately see Him as He is — in unveiled, radiant glory — and become like Him.

But what about those who reject Christ? What purpose does their future resurrection serve? It enables them to experience what they want — everlasting life on their own terms, apart from God. As Adam and Eve were banished from the presence of God in the Garden of Eden, so unbelievers are expelled from the new heavens and earth into what Jesus calls "outer darkness" (Matt. 25:30).

Jesus: firstborn and firstfruits

Our future resurrection is pinned to the resurrection of Jesus. King David prophesies that the grave cannot hold the coming Messiah (Ps. 16:10), a fact to which Peter and Paul attest as fulfilled in Jesus (Acts 2:24-36; 13:33-39). Jesus predicts His return from the grave (Matt. 12:39-40; 16:21; John 2:18-22), and this claim is common knowledge (Matt. 27:62-64). Jesus' bodily ascension into heaven is a foretaste of His personal, physical, and visible return one day (Acts 1:11).

As the resurrected Savior, Jesus is sometimes called the "firstborn" from the dead. The adjective *prototokos* (firstborn) is found nine times in the New Testament and is used in both literal and figurative senses. For example, a reference to Jesus as Mary's firstborn son appears in Luke 2:7. Meanwhile, Heb. 11:28 refers to the firstborn of Egyptian families that the avenging angel destroys.

But in metaphorical contexts, the meaning of "firstborn" signifies the person of Jesus Christ. Paul depicts Him as the firstborn of creation (Col. 1:15). This does not mean, as some suggest, that Jesus is a created being, for if Paul had intended that, he could have used the Greek word *protoktisis* (first-created) rather than *prototokos* (firstborn). Rather, the apostle is describing Jesus as "the initial representative of a regenerate communion of believers who would continue throughout eternity."[1]

In Rev. 1:5, John uses "firstborn from the dead" to exalt Jesus as the prime example of resurrected members of His body, the church. Put simply, Jesus is the foremost of those raised from the dead. Because of His physical resurrection, Jesus has been declared the powerful Son of God (Rom. 1:4), His work of redemption is complete, and we have the confident expectation of our own resurrection and glorification one day.

G.K. Beale notes that "firstborn" refers to the high, privileged position that Christ has as a result of His resurrection from the dead: "Christ has gained such a sovereign position over the cosmos, not in the sense that he is recognized as the first-created being of all creation or as the origin of creation, but in the sense that he is the inaugurator of the new creation by means of the resurrection."[2]

In addition to "firstborn," Jesus also is depicted as the "firstfruits." Like the first and best grain taken from the fields and offered to the Lord in the feast of firstfruits, Jesus is the first and best to pass through the vale of death and emerge victoriously, ensuring that the full harvest of believers is to be gathered one day.

The resurrection of Christians is pinned inextricably to the resurrection of Christ. As Paul writes, "For if the dead are not raised, Christ has not been raised. And if Christ has not been raised, your faith is worthless; you are still in your sins. Therefore, those who have fallen asleep in Christ have also perished. If we have put our hope in Christ for this life only, we should be pitied more than anyone. But now Christ has been raised from the dead, the firstfruits of those who have fallen asleep" (1 Cor. 15:16-20).

Jesus is both the firstborn and the firstfruits of the dead – the first to rise from the dead in glory, never to die again, and the foremost of those raised from the cold grip of the last enemy to be abolished: death (1 Cor. 15:26).

The believer's resurrection

It is comforting to keep in mind that when Christ died, He redeemed our bodies, souls, and spirits. Believers' salvation doesn't stop with the forgiveness of sins, the declaration of our right standing with God in Christ, and the sanctifying work of the Holy Spirit — although these are unfathomable gifts of grace. Rather, the redemptive work of Christ finds its ultimate fulfillment in future resurrection and glorification, when the effects of sin are completely removed, and believers are fully conformed to the image of Christ.

Equally comforting is the Lord's promise that neither death nor *Hades* threaten His children again. The apostle John, who hears Christ assure him that He holds the keys of death and *Hades*, later bears witness to the fact that these enemies are thrown into the lake of fire (Rev. 20:14). In our glorified bodies, we no longer sin, nor are we drawn to rebellion against God. As a resulting benefit, we have no reason to fear death, for it is but a distant memory God banishes from the realm of possibility.

One day Death and *Hades* are forced to give up their treasure. Christ uses His keys to open the graves and call the dead to life. *Hades* — the temporary abode of the dead — swallows the deceased no more. As the apostle Paul writes triumphantly for the believer: "For the Lord Himself will descend from heaven with a shout, with the archangel's voice, and with the trumpet of God, and the dead in Christ will rise first. Then we who are still alive will be caught up together with them in the clouds to meet the Lord in the air and so we will always be with the Lord. Therefore encourage one another with these words" (1 Thess. 4:16-18).

But how, exactly, does this work? Two passages of Scripture are most helpful in answering this question: 1 Cor. 15:50-58 and 1 Thess. 4:13-18. In these passages, Paul describes our future resurrection as a "mystery," or a secret hidden in the past but now revealed. In the resurrection of the just, Jesus descends from His throne in heaven and calls the "dead in Christ" to "rise first." The souls / spirits of the redeemed with Jesus in heaven are reunited with their resurrected bodies, which are "glorified," or made incorruptible and immortal. This happens in "the blink of an eye" and urges us to rejoice that death has been "swallowed up in victory."

Immediately after this, followers of Jesus who are alive and remain on the earth are caught up physically to "meet the Lord in the air." Their earthly bodies are instantly transformed into glorified bodies, without experiencing physical death. Both the resurrected saints and the living followers of Jesus who are "caught up together with them in the clouds" are assured that they will "always be with the Lord." Later, when Christ returns to earth, the glorified saints return with Him (1 Thess. 3:13; Rev. 19:14), along with the holy angels (Matt. 16:27; 2 Thess. 1:7).

What are these glorified bodies like? Paul uses differentiations within the created order as analogies for the similarities and differences between our earthly bodies and our resurrected ones (1 Cor. 15:35-44). For example, the wheat seed planted in the ground must die in order to spring to life with a stalk and heads of grain. There is continuity in kind — it remains wheat — but advancement in form.

In a similar manner, our earthly bodies are "sown in corruption, raised in incorruption." That is, our earthly bodies waste away and are prone to death, but our resurrected bodies are impervious to decay. Our earthly bodies are "sown in dishonor, raised in glory." This means, as Paul tells the Philippians, Christ "will transform the body of our humble condition into the likeness of His glorious body" (Phil. 3:21).

In addition, our earthly bodies are "sown in weakness, raised in power," another way of saying that our present inability to avoid all types of infirmities will give way to health and strength in glorification. Finally, our earthly bodies are "sown a natural body, raised a spiritual body." The bodies we now inhabit — animal-like, soulish — are incapable of perfect holiness, but our resurrected bodies are under the full control of the Holy Spirit.

Perhaps the best way to understand glorification is to examine the post-resurrection life of Jesus. He is raised in a physical body (John 2:18-22; Luke 24:39-40). He eats (Luke 24:41-43). He shows people His hands, feet, and side, complete with nail and spear prints in them (Luke 24:39; John 20:27).[3] People grab His feet and worship Him (Matt. 28:9). So, His resurrected body no doubt retains physical characteristics. At the same time, He is able to vanish from sight and appear in another place (Luke 24:31-36). He evidently is able to pass through locked doors (John 20:19). And He ascends into heaven (Acts 1:9).

While we struggle to fully understand the qualities of Jesus' resurrected body, we may rest assured that our glorified bodies are physical, fully controlled by the Spirit, and free of sin and its consequences. In essence, we are restored to the sinless perfection Adam and Eve enjoyed in the Garden, along with face-to-face fellowship with God.

The unbeliever's resurrection

There is less in Scripture about the resurrection of the wicked than there is about the glorification of the just. Nevertheless, the Bible gives us enough information to know that those who reject Christ are physically resurrected one day and separated forever from God.

Daniel gives us the clearest Old Testament glimpse of the resurrection of the wicked, and their everlasting destiny: "Many of those who sleep in the dust of the earth will awake, some to eternal life, and some to shame and eternal contempt" (Dan. 12:2). Job and Isaiah also offer insights into future resurrection (Job 19:25-27; Isa. 26:19).

In the New Testament, Jesus tells us that a day of reckoning is coming for all people — an event that begins with resurrection: "[A] time is coming when all who are in the graves will hear His voice and come out — those who have done good things, to the resurrection of life, but those who have done wicked things, to the resurrection of judgment" (John 5:28-29). The New Testament writers confirm final judgment of the wicked in numerous places, a judgment that presupposes resurrection (Acts 10:42; 17:31; 2 Thess. 1:6-9; Heb. 9:27; 1 Peter 4:5; 2 Peter 3:7).

We've surveyed the resurrection of life, also known as the "first resurrection" (Rev. 20:5-6). Let's look now at the resurrection of judgment, which leads to "the second death, the lake of fire" (Rev. 20:6, 14). It seems reasonable, but by no means certain, to conclude that the wicked of all ages are the last to be resurrected, depending on how one interprets Revelation 20. John writes, "The rest of the dead did not come to life until the 1,000 years were completed" (v. 5). These dead, great and small, stand before a great white throne and are judged according to their works (vv. 11-13).

Prior to this judgment, Satan is thrown into the lake of fire (v. 10). Presumably, demons are cast there at this time as well (Matt. 25:41). Then, Death and Hades are cast into hell (v. 14). This lends credence to the view that the wicked are the last to be resurrected because no one dies physically anymore

(Death), and there is no need for an intermediate abode of the dead (Hades). Last, the wicked, whose names are not found written in the book of life, are thrown into the lake of fire and experience the second death (v. 15).

But what kind of resurrected bodies do the wicked receive? Scripture offers no details like the ones Paul lays out for believers in 1 Corinthians 15. Even so, we may offer a few observations about the resurrected bodies of the damned:

- They are physical bodies, reunited with the souls / spirits of the wicked in *Hades*.

- They are fitted for everlasting separation from God in hell. Scripture does not support the false doctrine of annihilationism (see Chapter 7: Gehenna and the Afterlife for more details).

- They cannot be what Paul describes as "spiritual" bodies in 1 Cor. 15:44, for their owners have rejected Christ and thus are void of the indwelling Holy Spirit.

- They experience the second death — that is, the lake of fire — in which they are doomed forever for existence but not true life, for they are in outer darkness, cut off from the Source of Life.

What if there's no corpse?

Every person is physically resurrected one day, summoned before Christ on His throne of glory, and ushered into eternity, either in a glorified body similar to the body Christ had when He rose from the dead, or in a physical body prepared for everlasting existence in outer darkness.

What about those whose bodies have been cremated, lost at sea, ravaged in warfare, or otherwise ruined beyond recovery? The God who names the stars (Isa. 40:26) is fully capable of tracing every human atom and resurrecting every person ever conceived, and then fashioning that body for everlasting life with God or everlasting existence apart from Him.

Resurrection must take place for Christ to set things right. The salvation of believers depends on Jesus' finished work at Calvary, purging sin and its consequences from their whole being, and restoring in eternity what was sacrificed in time for His sake. A young woman beheaded for professing faith in Christ must experience the resurrection power of Jesus, whose brutalized body burst forth from the grave in health and wholeness. The child vanquished in his mother's womb, never allowed to draw his first breath, must experience the joys of childhood and the embrace of a loving Father. And the faithful bond-servant of Christ whose physical vigor erodes with the ravages of time must experience the vitality of being a new creation once again.

Equally important, the punishment of the wicked demands resurrection, for their sins are not confined to the soul. Jesus' story of Lazarus and the rich man illustrates the truth that we reap in eternity what we sow in time. In the resurrection of the wicked, the rich man, perhaps, will forever seek the creature comforts he denied Lazarus. The one who trafficked in human lives may find himself forever on the run as a marked man. And the false teacher who, for personal gain, proclaimed "another Jesus," "a different spirit," and "a different gospel" (2 Cor. 11:4), may find his sensual cravings forever unsatisfied, while he seeks to escape the haunting eyes of those he wooed into hell.

While outer darkness may seem unreasonably harsh, everyone who experiences everlasting existence apart from Christ has chosen it. The rich man in Jesus' parable confesses to being in torment, but he shows no willingness to repent of his sin (Luke 16:19-31). The resurrected wicked summoned before the great white throne watch in stunned silence as books are opened, revealing no evidence of a desire for Christ (Rev. 20:11-15). Even those who dare to offer a word in their own defense are proven to be lawbreakers whom Jesus never knew (Matt. 7:21-23).

When judgment falls on the wicked, it does not produce repentance, for that is the goal of God's kindness, restraint, and patience now (Rom. 2:4). In body and soul, the resurrected wicked remain, throughout eternity, what they have proven to be on this side of the grave.

Like a black hole, the second death sucks in everything in its path and permits no escape. The gentle touch of the Savior's hand, the still small voice calling the lost to repentance, the joy of an intimate relationship with the God of the universe — these have been rejected and are not welcome in the second death. Worse, there is no second chance. The second death — experienced in an indestructible body devoid of the Spirit — is final and irrevocable.

Think

Questions for personal or group study

What does it mean that Jesus is the "firstfruits of those who have fallen asleep" (1 Cor. 15:20)?

Why is the *physical* resurrection of Jesus important?

In what way is salvation incomplete without the resurrection?

How does the apostle Paul use a grain of wheat as an analogy for believers' present and future bodies (1 Cor. 15:35-38)?

How do the bodies of glorified saints differ from the bodies of resurrected unbelievers?

Based on Jesus' words in John 5:28-29, do you think everyone is resurrected and judged at the same time? Or, is it possible that time passes between the resurrection of life and the resurrection of judgment?

Why do you think the wicked need resurrected bodies?

Share

Talking points for discussing the resurrection

- The redemptive work of Christ finds its ultimate fulfillment in future resurrection and glorification, when the effects of sin are completely removed and believers are fully conformed to the image of Christ.

- Jesus is depicted in Scripture as the "firstfruits of those who have fallen asleep." Like the first and best grain taken from the fields and offered to the Lord in the feast of firstfruits, Jesus is the first and best to pass through the vale of death and emerge victoriously, ensuring that the full harvest of believers is to be gathered one day.

- Perhaps the best way to understand glorification is to examine the post-resurrection life of Jesus. He is raised in a physical body. Yet, He is able to do some amazing things, like pass through locked doors and ascend into heaven.

- While we struggle to fully understand the qualities of Jesus' resurrected body, we may rest assured that our glorified bodies are physical, fully controlled by the Spirit, and free of sin and its consequences.

- There is less in Scripture about the resurrection of the wicked than there is about the glorification of the just. Nevertheless, the Bible gives us enough information to know that those who reject Christ are physically resurrected one day and separated forever from God.

Our lifestyles *reflect* our beliefs. That is, our words and deeds reveal our citizenship, either in the kingdom of God or in the domain of the evil one.

six

Everyone's Day of Reckoning

One day, every person will be physically resurrected and summoned before Christ in final judgment. Jesus makes this plain. First, He declares that God the Father has entrusted all judgment to His Son (John 5:22). Then, He tells us about a future day of reckoning: "A time is coming when all who are in the graves will hear His voice and come out — those who have done good things, to the resurrection of life, but those who have done wicked things, to the resurrection of judgment" (John 5:28-29).

Some take this to mean that our destiny depends on us — our good works, or our evil deeds. However, this cannot be the case, for Jesus Himself sets the requirements for everlasting life in the very same context in which He speaks of future judgment. In John 5:24, He tells us, "Anyone who *hears* My word and *believes* Him who sent Me has eternal life and will not come under judgment but has passed from death to life" (John 5:24, emphasis added).

Further, the finished work of Christ, in which He took upon Himself our sins and paid the penalty for them on the cross, argues against works-based salvation (2 Cor. 5:21; Eph. 2:8-9; Titus 3:5). So, Jesus must be reminding us in John 5:28-29 that our lifestyles *reflect* our beliefs. That is, our words and deeds reveal our citizenship, either in the kingdom of God or in the domain of the evil one.

Even so, our works count for something. Heaven is not the same for every believer, nor do all those who reject Christ experience hell identically. Our final, personal, individual judgment before Christ is His way, as the righteous Judge, of setting things right for all eternity.

Our short stay on earth is a dress rehearsal for life beyond the grave. And one day, we all will stand before Jesus to give an account of what we did with the gospel, as well as our time, talents, opportunities, and other gifts of grace God has entrusted to us. The result is varying degrees of reward for believers, and varying degrees of punishment for unbelievers.

It's clear from Scripture that followers of Jesus stand in a different judgment than those who reject Christ. The apostle Paul tells us that Christians are summoned to the judgment seat of Christ (Rom. 14:10-12; 2 Cor. 5:10). At the same time, the apostle John is given a glimpse of the great white throne, upon which Jesus sits to judge those whose names are not written in the Lamb's book of life (Rev. 20:11-15).

The judgment seat of Christ

The judgment seat of Christ is the place where Christians, and perhaps believers of all ages, stand before Jesus to receive His evaluation of their lives. The result is everlasting reward, or the loss of reward, based on the degree of faithfulness to walk in the path of good works God set for them in eternity past (Eph. 2:10). Paul writes about this judgment in several places:

- Rom. 14:10-12: "But you, why do you criticize your brother? Or you, why do you look down on your brother? For we will all stand before the tribunal of God. For it is written: *As I live, says the Lord, every knee will bow to Me, and every tongue will give praise to God.* So then, each of us will give an account of himself to God."

- 1 Cor. 3:11-15: "For no one can lay any other foundation than what has been laid down. That foundation is Jesus Christ. If anyone builds on that foundation with gold, silver, costly stones, wood, hay, or straw, each one's work will become obvious, for the day will disclose it, because it will be revealed by fire; the fire will test the quality of each one's work. If anyone's work that he has built survives, he will receive a reward. If anyone's work is burned up, it will be lost, but he will be saved; yet it will be like an escape through fire."

- 2 Cor. 5:10: "For we must all appear before the tribunal of Christ, so that each may be repaid for what he has done in the body, whether good or worthless."

The Greek word translated "tribunal" (or "judgment seat" in some translations) is *bema*, a bench or platform from which public or judicial pronouncements are made. Pilate sits on the *bema* (Matt. 27:19; John 19:13), as do Herod (Acts 12:21) and

Gallio (Acts 18:12-17). Paul does not specify the exact time of this judgment. However, it seems reasonable to conclude that it is tied to our resurrection rather than to our death so that the full impact of our earthly lives — an impact that continues after our departure from earth — may be fully evaluated and rewarded.

This judgment does not determine a believer's eternal destiny, for that is fixed on this side of death with his or her decision to trust in Christ.

Rather, the *bema* judgment is where Christ rewards His followers based on how faithfully they managed the time, talents, spiritual gifts, and other good things they were given. Every Christian is a winner because Jesus has secured his or her eternal life through His finished work on the cross. But not every Christian is rewarded equally.

Jesus urges His followers to lay up treasure in heaven, where it is kept safe and endures (Matt. 6:20). The apostle Paul informs us that our works of faithfulness, which he likens to gold, silver, and precious stones, are refined in the fires of judgment and emerge purified (1 Cor. 3:11-15). And in the Book of Revelation, Jesus reminds us that our faithfulness is rewarded (Rev. 2:23; 22:12).

In fact, the New Testament mentions at least five "crowns," or rewards, believers may send ahead of them to heaven:

- The crown of righteousness, for those who love the appearing of Jesus and live as if He could return at any moment (2 Tim. 4:7-8)

- The incorruptible crown, for those who persevere in their Christian walk (1 Cor. 9:24-27)

- The crown of life, or the martyr's crown (Rev. 2:10)

- The crown of rejoicing, or the soul-winner's crown (1 Thess. 2:19-20)

- And the crown of glory, for those who shepherd the flock faithfully (1 Peter 5:1-4)

Why the *bema* judgment?

In 1 Cor. 4:1-5, Paul describes God's purpose for the *bema* judgment, as well as our proper perspective on it. "A person should consider us in this way: as servants of Christ and managers of God's mysteries," he writes. "In this regard, it is expected of managers that each one of them be found faithful…. The One who evaluates me is the Lord. Therefore don't judge anything prematurely, before the Lord comes, who will both bring to light what is hidden in darkness and reveal the intentions of the hearts. And then praise will come to each one from God."

This judgment is a full disclosure of our words and deeds, as Christ uncovers even our secret conversations, as well as our thoughts, intentions, and motivations. Like a purging fire, Christ's impartial evaluation of our lives burns away our worthless works and purifies our righteous ones. For the ones who have built well upon the foundation of their faith, they receive a "well done" from Christ and are given greater positions of authority and greater degrees of responsibility in His eternal kingdom (Matt. 25:21, 23).

Those who have squandered their Christian lives watch as their worthless works are consumed in the fires of judgment. Paul reminds such unfaithful believers, "If anyone's work is burned up, it will be lost, but he will be saved; yet it will be like an escape through fire" (1 Cor. 3:15). The apostle John warns his readers to remain faithful to Christ, lest they be ashamed at His coming (1 John 2:28).

"The judgment seat of Christ focuses on the assessment of a Christian's deeds or lifestyle rather than the determination of their eternal destiny," according to J. Daniel Hays, J. Scott Duvall, and C. Marvin Pate. "Having been saved by grace through faith (Eph. 2:8-9), Christians are nevertheless committed to working out their faith through deeds (e.g., Gal. 5:6; Eph. 2:10; Phil. 2:12-13; 1 Thess. 1:3). Believers are accountable for individual actions and are not exempt from doing good. Eschatology and ethics are bound tightly together. The judgment seat of Christ fulfills God's impartial justice, since not all believers live with the same degree of devotion to Christ. Christians are individually accountable for what they do in this mortal body."[1]

The great white throne

The great white throne, described in Rev. 20:11-15, is unique among the thrones of God in Scripture. It stands alone. It bears no context. It offers no hope, grace, or mercy. It calls no one to repentance. It prompts no one to sing. It fulfills no covenant promises. It surrounds itself with no rainbows, flaming torches, seas of glass, or heavenly creatures. It is perhaps the most solemn image of God's throne in the Bible, for it depicts the time and place where Christ — the Creator, Redeemer, and Judge — meets face to face with the wicked, who must now give an account of their lives. It is the last stop on the road to hell.

Joseph Seiss writes, "We read of no white robes, no spotless linen, no palms, nothing but naked sinners before the naked majesty of enthroned Almightiness, awaiting their eternal doom."[2]

As unbelievers stand before the great white throne — alone, without a defense, and with no escape — John notes that "books were opened. Another book was opened, which is the book of life, and the dead were judged according to their works by what was written in the books" (Rev. 20:12). What are these books, and how many are there? What is different about the book of life that it should be named, while the others are mentioned as a group without distinction?

It seems clear that God keeps a record of our lives and holds us accountable for how we manage the time, talents, relationships, and other gifts He has entrusted to us. He knows our thoughts, which form the action plans for good and evil deeds (see, for example, Matt. 5:27-28). He hears our words, which reveal the true nature of our hearts and for which we must give an account (Matt. 12:33-37).

In various places, the Bible depicts God's record of our lives as contained in heavenly books. No person escapes the Creator's interest or avoids a day of reckoning with Him. "Myriads of human beings have lived and died of whom the world knows nothing; but the lives they lived, the deeds they wrought, the thoughts and tempers they indulged, still stand written where the memory of them cannot perish. Not a human being has ever breathed earth's atmosphere whose career is not traced at full length in the books of eternity."[3]

The books that record the unbelievers' deeds are opened in order to show them at least two truths: the full extent of their lifelong wickedness, and the failure of their good deeds to earn the favor of God.

The book of life

In addition, there is a search for their names in the book of life, where their eternal bliss in the presence of Christ may have been secured by faith. But no, their names are not to be found. As a result, they are banished to outer darkness, or hell.

What's so special about the book of life? Its pages list no good deeds, no legacy of charitable acts, no meritorious service worthy of everlasting life. So, it seems there is no reason the names of the wicked are excluded. If they could scour the pages, they would see the names of people great and small — leaders, foot soldiers, neighbors, family members. To the mind of the damned, the listing makes no sense.

There is ample room in the book for every person's name, and yet their names are missing. Why? An entry in this book is not achieved through human effort but through simple surrender. Those written in the book of life have washed their robes in the blood of the Lamb, and He has written their names with His own blood. Those who would not have the Lamb will not have life. They are thrown into the lake of fire. The difference is that the wicked have pleaded their own righteousness while the righteous have pleaded the blood of the Lamb.

There are no doubt degrees of punishment in hell just as there are varying rewards in heaven. Eternity in hell is not the same for the mass murderer as for the law-abiding citizen, but it is outer darkness nonetheless.

Jesus saves some of His most graphic depictions of the darkness and loneliness of hell for the most religious of His day. He tells the Jewish leaders they will receive greater condemnation because they know the Scriptures, which point to Jesus, yet persist in their hypocritical and destructive work against the kingdom of God (Matt. 23:14). He tells the story of Lazarus and the rich man in front of the Pharisees to illustrate that wealth and privilege are not the entitlements God owes a righteous person; rather, heaven awaits those who humbly trust in Him for salvation (Luke 16:19-31).

What a comfort it is for believers to know their names are written in the book of life, and what a shock it must be for countless unbelievers who discover before the great white throne that their names are absent from heaven's roll. On earth their deeds earned a place in many great books — books of valor, conquest, heroics, feats, discoveries, inventions, charities, religious quests, political coups, scientific breakthroughs, medical advances, social progress, military campaigns, community activism, and legendary leadership.

Perhaps their names are inscribed on grand buildings, or chiseled into monuments, or painted on the hulls of ocean-going vessels. At the very least the newspapers noticed their entrance into the world — and their departure from it. Somewhere, their names are inscribed in family trees or scribbled in the opening pages of family Bibles. How can it be that the God who created all people does not ensure that their names are in His book of life?

There must be some mistake. "Lord, Lord, didn't we prophesy in Your name?" some cry out. "Didn't we drive out demons in your name, and do many miracles in Your name?" The One seated on the throne does not deny they invoked His name on numerous occasions, no doubt producing some earthly good. But He reveals there is no relationship between them when He utters the seven most tragic words in human history: "Depart from Me, I never knew you" (Matt. 7:23 KJV).

Anyone not found

Rev. 20:15 is as clear as Scripture can be: "And anyone not found written in the book of life was thrown into the lake of fire."

There is but one way a person's name is entered into the book of life: God writes it there and never blots it out. Just as He chooses believers in Christ from the foundation of the world, He keeps those who belong to Him and never lets them go.

Many debate whether God's election is anchored simply in divine foreknowledge, or in hard determinism, or even fatalism. No doubt, much about the will of God is beyond our understanding. Yet it appears that God's sovereignty encompasses His decision to entrust all people with the ability to make choices for which He holds them responsible. No one is denied a place in the book of life, and no one's name is entered there beyond their assent.

As the wicked pass through the gates of hell in Dante's epic poem *Inferno*, they are greeted with these words: "Abandon hope, all you who enter here." They remind the damned that once inside, there is no escape from the fiery torments they have brought upon themselves.

As Charles Swindoll writes, "Though the details of Dante's fictional picture of heaven, hell, and purgatory range from the fantastic to the heretical, he was right about this: the final destination of the wicked features a one-way entrance. All hope vanishes beyond; there will be no escape from the lake of fire…. The facts of eternal punishment are set forth without a hint of hope … because no hope exists apart from God."[4]

Every knee will bow

Paul writes to the Philippians that one day "every knee will bow — of those who are in heaven and on earth and under the earth — and every tongue should confess that Jesus Christ is Lord, to the glory of God the Father" (Phil. 2:10-11). Believers' knees bow in humble adoration, and any crowns placed upon their heads are cast at Jesus' feet. Unbelievers' knees bow in grudging acknowledgement that while they will have their way and live forever apart from Jesus, He is the ultimate Master with the authority to rule over the human heart.

It is a common expression at funerals that the deceased have "gone on to their eternal reward." Meant to comfort mourners that their loved ones are "in a better place," the statement glosses over the deeper truth that indeed all people ultimately are repaid for their lives on earth.

The "reward" may be our Savior's greeting, "Come, you who are blessed by My Father, inherit the kingdom prepared for you from the foundation of the world" (Matt. 25:34), followed by the bliss of authority and responsibility in the presence of the Lord in the new heavens and new earth.

Or, the "reward" may be the words of the One seated on the throne of His glory: "Depart from Me, You who are cursed, into the eternal fire prepared for the Devil and his angels!" (Matt. 25:41).

Ultimately, everyone gets the eternal destiny they choose, based on their acceptance or rejection of Christ. In addition, everyone spends eternity as close to, or as far away from, their Creator as they desire based on how they lived out their acceptance or rejection of the Savior.

Jesus reminds us in the Book of Revelation that when He returns, He will set things right: "Look! I am coming quickly, and My reward is with Me to repay each person according to what he has done" (Rev. 22:12). His words should prompt all people to search their hearts and take stock of their treasure.

Think

If salvation is by grace alone, through faith alone, in Christ alone, why do our works matter?

Is it possible that hell won't be so bad for the moral person who never trusted in Christ?

Why doesn't Jesus take away the salvation of a Christian who has nothing good to show on judgment day?

Why do you think the New Testament depicts rewards for Christians as crowns?

How does the concept of rewards and punishments help us understand the justice of God?

Is it fair for Jesus to send people to hell who never heard of Him? Why or why not?

Why do you think we stand in final judgment after our resurrection, which could be hundreds of years from now, rather than immediately after our death?

Share

- One day, every person will be physically resurrected and summoned before Christ in final judgment.

- Most scholars believe the judgment seat of Christ is the place where Christians, and perhaps believers of all ages, stand before Jesus to receive His evaluation of their lives, resulting in everlasting reward or loss of reward based on the degree of their faithfulness to walk in the path of good works God set for them in eternity past.

- Unbelievers of all times will stand one day before the great white throne. There, it will be shown that their names are absent from the book of life. They will be given varying degrees of punishment in hell.

- There are no doubt degrees of punishment in hell just as there are varying rewards in heaven. Eternity in hell is not the same for the mass murderer as for the law-abiding citizen, but it is outer darkness nonetheless.

- It seems clear that God keeps a record of our lives and holds us accountable for how we manage the time, talents, relationships, and other gifts He has entrusted to us. He knows our thoughts, which form the action plans for good and evil deeds. He hears our words, which reveal the true nature of our hearts and for which we must give an account.

seven
Gehenna and the Afterlife

The ultimate destiny of the wicked is the same habitation created for Satan and his demons — a place in English we call "hell," and a place Jesus and the New Testament writers describe variously as *Gehenna*, "outer darkness," "eternal fire," "eternal punishment," "lake of fire," and "the second death."

While *Sheol* and *Hades* generally depict the temporary abode of the dead, *Gehenna* and its associated terms describe the place of everlasting future punishment for those whose names are not written in the book of life (Rev. 20:15).

The term *Gehenna* is derived from the Valley of Hinnom. Located southwest of Jerusalem, this steep, rocky valley is the scene of human sacrifices to pagan deities (2 Kings 23:10; 2 Chron. 28:3; 33:6), and Jeremiah declares it the "Valley of Slaughter" (Jer. 7:31-34).

To the Jewish mind, the images of fire and destruction become appropriate representations of the ultimate fate of idol worshipers.

How Jesus depicts *Gehenna*

Jesus seizes rabbinic language connected with *Gehenna*, such as "unquenchable fire" and "never-dying worms," to impress upon His listeners that their choices in this life have everlasting consequences. In fact, of the 12 uses of *Gehenna* in the New Testament, 11 come from the lips of the Messiah.

It's probable that Jesus uses *Gehenna* on only four occasions: In the Sermon on the Mount (Matt. 5:22, 29, 30); in warning the disciples not to fear men (Matt. 10:28; Luke 12:5); in a discourse on relationships (Matt. 18:9; Mark 9:43, 45, 47); and in His denunciation of the scribes and Pharisees (Matt. 23:15, 33).

Traditionally, these passages are understood to speak of final judgment, with Jesus using images from everyday life to warn about a place of everlasting separation from God.[1]

However, some scholars see Jesus speaking in more limited terms. Steve Gregg, in *All You Want to Know About Hell: Three Christian Views of God's Final Solution to the Problem of Sin*, argues that Jesus may have used *Gehenna* literally to warn first-century Jews that they are about to suffer fiery judgment for their rejection of the Messiah at the hands of the Romans — a judgment that falls hard on Jerusalem and its inhabitants in A.D. 70.[2]

This is not to deny the existence of hell as a place of everlasting separation from God, since other texts speak of resurrection, final judgment, and fiery punishment for the wicked. But it is to encourage us to carefully consider the context so we do not glean more from a text than is warranted.

Is hell forever?

Anglican cleric John Stott, who wrote the influential book *Basic Christianity*, found the idea of eternal suffering in hell so repugnant that he rejected it in favor of annihilationism.

Those who embrace the idea of body and soul ceasing to exist after spending some amount of time in hell point out that the "fire" and "worms" to which Jesus refers are indeed eternal, but the body and soul are destroyed. Two responses are offered.

First, the rabbinic understanding of these terms is that the bodies and souls of the wicked are eternal, not just the fires and worms, according to Robert Morey in *Death and the Afterlife*.

Second, the term "destroyed" in Matt. 10:28 does not mean annihilated. As *Thayer's Greek-English Lexicon* defines the word *apollumi*, it means "to be delivered up to eternal misery." In every instance where the word *apollumi* is found in the New Testament, something other than annihilation is described, writes Morey.[3]

For example, people do not pass into nonexistence when they become hungry (Luke 15:17), and wineskins don't vanish into thin air when they burst (Matt. 9:17). In each of these instances, the writers use the term *apollumi*.

While rejecting annihilationism, other Christian leaders favor a form of universalism that requires suffering in hell as a prerequisite for heaven.

But Jesus' teachings on "outer darkness," "eternal fire," and "eternal punishment" seem to support the concept of *Gehenna* as a place of conscious, everlasting separation from God.

Hell's inhabitants

It's important to note *who* and *what* are cast into the lake of fire: The beast and the false prophet (Rev. 19:20); Satan (20:10); anyone whose name is not found written in the book of life (20:15); cowards, unbelievers, the vile, murderers, the sexually immoral, sorcerers, idolaters, and all liars — meaning the unrepentant wicked (21:8); and ultimately Death and Hades (20:14).

The fires of hell devour all wicked humans and spirits, and even the consequences of sin — death and temporary disembodiment for the deceased. As the apostle Paul writes, those who don't know God and those who do not obey the gospel "will pay the penalty of eternal destruction from the Lord's presence ..." (2 Thess. 1:9).

Perhaps this divine act of judgment is the first step in what Peter describes as God's work of creating new heavens and a new earth (2 Peter 3:10-13).

Fire and darkness

Finally, are we to take the lake of fire literally or figuratively? Godly scholars stand on both sides of the debate.

It may help to remember that the Bible uses fire metaphorically many times. Daniel sees the throne of God in heaven as "flaming fire; its wheels were blazing fire" (Dan. 7:9). James describes the tongue as an appendage that "sets the course of life on fire, and is set on fire by hell" (James 3:6).

So, it may be that the Bible's depiction of hell in such graphic terms is God's way of explaining an indescribable place in language we can understand.

Whether literal or metaphorical, the fires of hell are to be avoided at all costs, and the blood of Jesus is to be pleaded for forgiveness of sins while there is yet time.

Think

Questions for personal or group study

What terms besides *Gehenna* do Jesus and the New Testament writers use to describe the eternal destiny of the wicked?

Do you think it's fair for God to punish someone eternally for sins committed in a single lifetime? Which passages of Scripture support your point of view?

Why do you think Jesus speaks so frequently about hell in the New Testament?

Who ultimately ends up in hell?

How does a person avoid hell?

What are the arguments in favor of annihilationism? Universalism? How might you respond biblically?

Share

Talking points for discussing *Gehenna* and the afterlife

- The ultimate destiny of the wicked is the same habitation created for Satan and his demons — a place in English we call "hell," and a place Jesus and the New Testament writers describe variously as *Gehenna*, "outer darkness," "eternal fire," "eternal punishment," "lake of fire," and "the second death."

- The term *Gehenna* is derived from the Valley of Hinnom — the scene of human sacrifices to pagan deities in Old Testament times.

- Jesus seizes rabbinic language connected with *Gehenna*, such as "unquenchable fire" and "never-dying worms," to impress upon His listeners that their choices in this life have everlasting consequences.

- While some argue for annihilationism or universalism, Jesus' teachings on "outer darkness," "eternal fire," and "eternal punishment" seem to support the concept of *Gehenna* as a place of conscious, everlasting separation from God.

- Whether literal or metaphorical, the fires of hell are to be avoided at all costs, and the blood of Jesus is to be pleaded for forgiveness of sins while there is yet time.

Let's consider for a moment that the notion of a loving God and the doctrine of hell are perfectly compatible. There is nothing of one that cancels out the other.

eight

The Goodness of Hell

One of the most disturbing truths of the Christian faith is the doctrine of hell. Atheists use it to deny the existence of a loving God. And Christians find themselves squeamishly defending the notion that a good God sends some people to a place of everlasting torment.

"Hell is of course the greatest evil of all, the realm of the greatest conceivable suffering," writes Christian author Dinesh D'Souza in *God Forsaken*. "Consequently, hell poses perhaps the deepest difficulty for Christian theodicy [an attempt to reconcile the goodness of God with the existence of evil]. Far from resolving the theodicy problem, hell seems to make it even worse."[1]

Atheist Robert Ingersoll asserted that hell "makes man an eternal victim and God an eternal fiend."[2]

Anglican cleric John Stott, who wrote the influential book *Basic Christianity*, found the idea of eternal suffering so repugnant that he rejected it in favor of annihilationism.[3]

Even C.S. Lewis shuddered at the concept of hell: "There is no doctrine which I would more willingly remove from Christianity than this, if it lay in my power."[4]

The goodness of hell

But let's consider for a moment that the notion of a loving God and the doctrine of hell are perfectly compatible. There is nothing of one that cancels out the other.

Jesus spoke frequently on hell and alluded to it in parables. He used the word *Gehenna*, derived from the Valley of Hinnom outside Jerusalem, where apostate Israelites in Old Testament times sacrificed their children to false gods.

Jesus told some religious leaders they were headed for hell. He warned His listeners against this place where the worm does not die and the fires are not quenched. He referred to hell as "outer darkness." And He said hell was created for Satan and demons, yet made it clear that many people will spend eternity there.

So, in what possible way is hell good?

First, hell is good because it affirms God's justice. If God only had the qualities of benevolence and mercy, hell would be an unreasonable place. But God is infinitely holy and perfectly just. To sin against Him offends His very nature.

Human beasts like Hitler, Stalin, and Pol Pot are responsible for the slaughter of millions of people whose lives ended in starvation, torture, human experimentation, or execution. How can the mere death of these tyrants by any means satisfy justice?

If we accept the doctrine of universalism, we must admit that Osama bin Laden and Mother Teresa are feasting at the same banquet table. Without the existence of hell, life indeed is cruel and life's Creator is eternally unjust.

Second, hell is good because it affirms free will. While we may debate whether humans truly have free will, or simply make decisions within pre-determined boundaries, there is little question that God allows us to make choices for which we are held accountable. In a world where God refuses to grant humans real choices, there is no freedom to love God.

If we view life fatalistically, God is a cruel puppet master who manipulates us before discarding us like broken toys. But the biblical concept of hell carries with it the clear teaching that people choose to spend eternity apart from Christ. As C.S. Lewis so poignantly penned, "[T]he doors of Hell are locked on the inside."[5]

Without hell, our choices have no real meaning or lasting consequences.

Third, hell is good because it implies heaven. Many atheists attack the idea that a good God would send people to hell for eternity as payment for temporal sins. But they tend not to criticize the idea of a God who welcomes people into eternal bliss merely for being the recipients of His grace.

Freud argued that heaven is a product of wishful thinking. But if that's so, how does one explain the fact that religions embracing heaven also have clear doctrines of hell?

We are invited to join God in this life and the life to come by His grace through faith. We may reject Him and enter eternity on our own terms, but we cannot take God with us or it would cease to be hell.

Outer darkness

While it is troubling to consider eternity in "outer darkness," the Bible is clear that hell is a place people choose to live independently of God — forever.

We do not see the rich man repent of his sin in Luke 16, nor do we see those before the great white throne asking to be near Jesus (Rev. 20:11-15); indeed, the blasphemers and unrepentant in Revelation hide themselves from the presence of God, preferring death under a rock to life in the light of Christ.

A final caution: When we say hell is good, we do not mean to gloat over those who enter eternity without Christ, no matter how wicked they may be. The Lord Himself does not delight in the judgment of the ungodly but took the human condition so seriously He sent His Son to save us from ourselves.

Think

Questions for personal or group study

Why do you think people go to hell if Jesus said hell was created for Satan and demons (Matt. 25:41)?

Do you think it's possible that hell is a place of temporary suffering rather than a place of everlasting conscious existence apart from God? How does Scripture support your point of view?

How might you reconcile the seemingly conflicting depiction of hell as a place of both fire and darkness?

Do you think it's possible for people in hell to repent of their sins and become truly remorseful over their rejection of God? Why or why not?

What problems do you see in Christian universalism (the belief that God ultimately redeems all people)? What are the strengths and weaknesses of annihilationism (the belief that the wicked cease to exist rather than suffer everlastingly in hell)?

Share

Talking points for discussing the goodness of hell

- The notion of a loving God and the doctrine of hell are perfectly compatible. There is nothing of one that cancels out the other.

- Hell is good because it affirms God's justice. Without the existence of hell, life indeed is cruel and life's Creator is eternally unjust.

- Hell is good because it affirms free will. Without hell, our choices have no real meaning or lasting consequences.

- Hell is good because it implies heaven. If there is a place of eternal separation from God, there also must be a place of everlasting intimacy with Him.

- The Lord does not delight in the judgment of the ungodly but took the human condition so seriously He sent His Son to save us from ourselves.

nine

Is Heaven Our Final Home?

Is heaven the final destination of all who rest in Jesus? Or do we spend eternity someplace else?

In 2 Corinthians 5, the apostle Paul describes two different states of existence for the Christian. While we are "at home in the body we are away from the Lord." And when we are "out of the body" we are "at home with the Lord" (5:6, 8).

Let's unpack this marvelous truth. The New Testament teaches that upon death, believers' souls/spirits separate from our lifeless bodies and enter the presence of God in heaven (see also Phil. 1:21-24). There we enjoy intimate fellowship with our Lord while awaiting the future resurrection and glorification of our bodies (John 5:28-29; 1 Cor. 15:51-58; 1 Thess. 4:13-18).

We see magnificent glimpses into the throne room of heaven through the visionary eyes of the apostle John in the Book of Revelation: the triune Godhead; an emerald-colored rainbow surrounding a glorious throne; living creatures; elders; angels; and redeemed people from every tribe, language, people, and nation. The combined voices of all creatures in heaven, on earth, under the earth, and in the sea proclaim, "Blessing and honor and glory and dominion to the One seated on the throne, and to the Lamb, forever and ever!" (Rev. 5:13).

We may be tempted to stop here, as if heaven is the final destination in life's long journey. It *is* breathtaking. But it gets better. Heaven, a place so awe-inspiring that Paul is not allowed to speak the inexpressible words he hears while visiting there, nevertheless is a temporary home for those who rest in the Lord until He returns to earth and brings us with Him.

As Randy Alcorn writes, "The intermediate Heaven is *not* our final destination. Though it will be a wonderful place, the intermediate Heaven is not the place we were made for — the place God promises to refashion on a resurrected Earth. We must not lose sight of our true destination. If we do, we'll be confused and disoriented in our thinking about where, and in what form, we will spend eternity."[1]

What should we know, then, about heaven?

Three heavens

While rabbis in ancient times envisioned as many as seven heavens, the Bible generally uses the Hebrew word *shamayim* and the Greek word *ouranos* in three ways:

1. The atmospheric heaven, or the sky (Gen. 1:8). It's where the birds fly (Mark 4:32), the clouds carry storms (Luke 12:56), and the rain falls (James 5:18).

2. The stellar heaven(s), where the moon and stars shine (Ps. 8:3; Heb. 11:12).

3. And the domain of God, or His dwelling place (1 Kings 22:19; Luke 20:4).

The Scriptures also speak of the "heavens" as a metaphor for where Christ reigns with His church (Eph. 2:6), as well as the unseen spiritual realm inhabited by evil beings (Eph. 6:12). The context determines the proper meaning of the word.

For the purposes of this brief study, we are concerning ourselves with what the apostle Paul calls the "third heaven," or "paradise," the domain of God (2 Cor. 12:2). It is the intermediate state between death and resurrection for Christians, giving way ultimately to everlasting life on a restored earth.

What about heaven?

The New Testament reveals many truths about this intermediate state for followers of Jesus:

- The Father, Son, and Holy Spirit reside in heaven, yet they have immediate access to earth (Matt. 3:16-17).

- God's will is done completely in heaven — and one day will be done on earth (Matt. 6:9-10).

- Angels surround the throne in heaven (Matt. 18:10), as do majestic heavenly creatures and redeemed people (Revelation 4-5).

- The heavenly throne is the heart of God's authority and majesty (Mark 16:19).

- Heaven is the place from which Satan fell and has no future part (Luke 10:18; Rev. 20:10).

- Heaven is where believers' names are written down, providing assurance of everlasting life (Luke 10:20; Heb. 12:23).

- Christ is preparing a place for believers in heaven and will take us there one day (John 14:1-3), bringing us back to earth with Him when He returns (Rev. 19:11-16).

- Our citizenship is in heaven (Phil. 3:20-21).

- Our inheritance is in heaven — imperishable, uncorrupted, and unfading (1 Peter 1:4).

- Jesus came from heaven (John 3:31; 6:38, 42), ascended there after His finished work on the cross (Luke 24:51; Eph. 4:10; Heb. 4:14); and will descend from heaven one day to resurrect and glorify believers (1 Thess. 4:16-17; 1 Cor. 15:51-58).

- God brings heaven and earth together one day and dwells with us (Rev. 21:3-4).

- Nothing profane enters heaven — or the new heavens and new earth (Rev. 21:27 – 22:5).

Better by far

As wonderful as the intermediate heaven is, our ultimate destiny is the new heavens and new earth, which Peter and John describe as a place of righteousness and restored innocence (2 Peter 3:10-13; Revelation 21-22). Christ returns, resurrects and judges all people, establishes His kingdom in fullness, creates new heavens and a new earth, and gives us roles to play in the administration of His kingdom.

The Greek word John uses for "new" in Rev. 21:1 is *kainos*, which means "different from the usual, impressive, better than the old, superior in value or attraction."[2] In other words, God does not annihilate the old order of things and start again from scratch; He purges the sinful and fallen cosmos and restores it to its pristine beauty. Jesus calls this work "the regeneration" of the earth, or "the Messianic Age" (Matt. 19:28). Peter explains it as a cleansing and renewing by fire (2 Peter 3:10-13).

The new heavens and new earth stand in stark contrast to Eden after the Fall. God is fully revealed, and we are glorified so that our natural desire is for the intimacy Adam and Eve experienced in the garden. God sets His throne among us, and we do not flee from His presence with the shame that drove Adam and Eve to hide among the trees. There is personal contact with our sovereign Creator. We call Him *Abba* — dearest Daddy — and He calls us His children. There is security, warmth, serenity, joy, and unending peace. God is with us and we never again experience the consequences of separation from the One who is our life.

While the intermediate heaven is the joyous aim of all who trust in Jesus, the new heavens and new earth are better by far.

Satan, sin, and death — three enemies that Christ conquered through His finished work on the cross — are banished to the lake of fire, along with all those who reject God's provision for eternal life. God wipes the tears from His children's cheeks and declares that the former things — death, grief, crying, and pain — have passed away.

J.I. Packer writes, "As life in the 'intermediate' or 'interim' state between death and resurrection is better than life in this world that preceded it, so the life of resurrection will be better still. It will, in fact, be best. And this is what God has in store for all his children."[3]

Amen. Come, Lord Jesus.

Think

Why is heaven not the final destiny of Christians?

How does Revelation 4-5 give us a glimpse of what heaven is like?

What are the different ways the word "heaven" is used in the New Testament?

Where do you think heaven is? Is it a place, a state of being, or something different altogether?

Who and what have no place in heaven?

How does the intermediate heaven relate to the new heavens and new earth?

Share

Talking points for discussing heaven

- At death, believers' souls/spirits separate from our lifeless bodies and enter the presence of God in heaven, where we enjoy intimate fellowship with our Lord while awaiting the future resurrection and glorification of our bodies.

- Heaven is not believers' final destination; when Christ returns to earth, we return with Him and serve Him in the new heavens and the new earth.

- Generally, the Bible uses the term "heaven" in three ways: the atmospheric heaven (sky), the stellar heavens (space), and the domain of God (throne). The context determines the meaning.

- To create new heavens and new earth, God does not annihilate the old order of things and start again from scratch; He purges the sinful and fallen cosmos and restores it to its pristine beauty.

- While the intermediate heaven is the joyous aim of all who trust in Jesus, the new heavens and new earth are better by far.

ten
A Look into Tartarus

If *Sheol / Hades* is the temporary abode of deceased people, is there a transitory place of punishment for some demons? It seems the answer is yes, in a place the New Testament refers to as *Tartarus*.

The New Testament mentions *Tartarus* only once, in 2 Peter 2:4. Many translations render it "hell," including the King James Version and the New American Standard Bible, while others, like the English Standard Version and the New International Version, provide footnotes linking the English word "hell" to the Greek name *Tartarus*.

The Holman Christian Standard Bible simply transliterates the Greek word in this passage, which reads: "For if God didn't spare the angels who sinned but threw them down into *Tartarus* and delivered them to be kept in chains of darkness until judgment ..."

A footnote in the HCSB reads: "*Tartarus* is a Greek name for a subterranean place of divine punishment lower than *Hades*."[1]

In the apocryphal Book of Enoch (20:2), *Tartarus* is a place where fallen angels are punished, an interpretation Peter affirms.

So, *Tartarus* seems to be a place separate from *Sheol*, the Hebrew term for the abode of the dead; *Hades*, roughly the Greek equivalent of *Sheol*; and *Gehenna*, the lake of fire created for the Devil and his angels (Matt. 25:41), where wicked people also spend eternity (Rev. 20:15).

Ancient Greeks regarded *Tartarus* as a place where rebellious gods and other wicked ones are punished. Peter refers to *Tartarus* as the abode of certain fallen angels.

Pits of darkness

Peter reminds us that while Satan's ultimate destiny is hell, currently he is free, roaming the earth like a lion, looking for anyone he can devour (1 Peter 5:8). In a similar fashion, many of his demons are free — tempting, tormenting, and even possessing individuals.

At the same time, the New Testament teaches that some fallen angels experience incarceration and conscious torment as they await the Day of Judgment.

Note first of all in 2 Peter 2:4 that God has cast some angels into *Tartarus*, committing them to "pits of darkness" or, as some translations render it, "chains of darkness." This Jewish apocalyptic phrase refers to a place of mental anguish and terror in the underworld.

Second, these angels are confined until the Day of Judgment. The word "confined" is in the present passive participle tense, meaning they are continually kept or reserved for judgment.

We find a similar passage in Jude 6, where we read God has "kept, with eternal chains in darkness for the judgment of the great day, the angels who did not keep their own position ..."

We should note there may be other places of confinement for demons. For example, demons possessing the man called Legion beg Jesus not to banish them to the "abyss," an unfathomable pit mentioned nine times in the New Testament. In Revelation 9, 11, 17, and 20, we see that an angel called Destroyer rules over the abyss; that it is a fiery place kept under lock and key; that the beast is released from the abyss to foment great wickedness on the earth; and that Satan is temporarily imprisoned there.

Finally, in Rev. 9:14, an angel is commanded to release four demons confined at the Euphrates River.

A dark recess of hell?

We might ask: Is *Tartarus* an especially dark recess of hell, or a separate temporary abode until the final judgment of Satan and his demons?

If *Tartarus* is a compartment of hell, then why are demons kept there until judgment day, only to be returned? Why are some demons released from imprisonment in the abyss and at the Euphrates River, while those in *Tartarus* are offered no parole?

Finally, if there is no escape from *Tartarus*, how does this place of temporary confinement differ from the lake of fire?

While we may ponder these issues, it's always good to stick with what the Bible clearly teaches. First, Christ has defeated Satan, sin, and death for people; there is no redemption for the angels who rebelled. Second, Christ judges angels as well as people. And third, we may rest assured that Satan and all his demons have a place prepared for them — the lake of fire — where they will be cast one day and tormented forever.

If some especially vile fallen angels are kept in a temporary place called *Tartarus* and never allowed to carry out their evil intentions, so much the better for us.

Think

Questions for personal or group study

Why do you think some demons are free and others are confined?

What is the difference between *Tartarus* and the abyss?

If there is no reprieve from *Tartarus*, why didn't God just send the demons directly to hell? What difference do you think the Day of Judgment makes for them?

What are some ways the Bible describes the work of Satan and demons in the world today?

Why has God provided redemption for sinful people but not for Satan and demons?

Share

Talking points for discussing *Tartarus* and the afterlife

- *Tartarus* is a Greek name for a subterranean place of divine punishment lower than *Hades*. Peter and Jude write that it is a place where certain demons are confined until the Day of Judgment.

- Today, Satan and many demons are free, while others are confined. But the ultimate destiny of all fallen angels is the lake of fire, which God created for them (Matt. 25:41).

- In contrast to *Tartarus*, which is a place of permanent confinement, some demons are imprisoned temporarily in the abyss or at the Euphrates River, according to Scripture.

- While there is no redemption for Satan and demons, Christ has conquered Satan, sin, and death for fallen human beings, and by His grace through faith we may receive everlasting life.

- If some especially vile fallen angels are kept in a temporary place called *Tartarus* and never allowed to carry out their evil intentions, so much the better for us.

eleven
Should You Believe in Ghosts?

Ghosts are everywhere. They star in major motion pictures from *The Shining* to *Scary Movie 2*. Some ghosts are friendly (Casper), and some are frightening (Bloody Mary).

Popular television shows like *Ghost Adventures* use the latest technologies to "prove" that spirits of the dead are all around us — and want to make their presence known.

But is this true? The short answer is no. As Christians, we must gauge all truth claims by the Bible, the ultimate and unchanging measure of reality.

Ghost stories in the Gospels

Some people argue that the apostles believed in ghosts and even thought Jesus was one when He walked toward their boat on the Sea of Galilee (Matt. 14:22-33).

Later, after Christ's resurrection, the apostles once again mistook Jesus for a ghost. He assured them that "a ghost does not have flesh and bones as you can see I have" (Luke 24:39).

Don't the beliefs of the apostles and the words of Jesus prove that ghosts are all around us?

Let's be clear on two points. First, Scripture teaches that all humans possess both physical and non-physical properties — the body and the soul/spirit, the second of which survives physical death.

Second, nowhere does the Bible support the notion that spirits of the dead (*phantasma* or *pneuma* in the Greek) are free to return to the physical realm prior to their future resurrection.

In other words, the departed are just that: departed.

Heaven or Hades

The souls of the dead either are in the presence of God in heaven or separated from Him in torment in *Hades*.

In Jesus' story of Lazarus and the rich man, the righteous beggar at death is carried by the angels to Abraham's side and is comforted there, while the unrighteous aristocrat finds himself in torment beyond the grave.

The rich man petitions Abraham to send Lazarus to warn his brothers, but Abraham makes it clear that is not permitted: "They have Moses and the prophets; they should listen to them" (Luke 16:29).

The apostle Paul reminds us that when Christians die, their souls/spirits go directly into the presence of God (2 Cor. 5:8).

The appearances of the righteous dead on earth are brief and rare exceptions to the rule. For example, Moses and Elijah appear briefly on the Mount of Transfiguration with Jesus and His inner circle of apostles (Matt. 17:1-9).

In the Old Testament, we read the story of Samuel, who appears on earth after his death. King Saul has gone to the witch of Endor, seeking to engage her in necromancy — communicating with the dead, a practice denounced in Scripture and banished by fiat from the land of Israel in Saul's day.

The appearance of Samuel shocks the witch as much as it surprises Saul. As Hank Hanegraaff describes it, "When the departed Samuel appeared to the living Saul, the witch of Endor immediately recognized the occasion as a non-normative act of God — a divine display of judgment rather than a haunting."[1]

In other words, God called the witch's bluff. She dabbled in deception and demonic activity to ply her trade but had no real power to bring back the spirits of the dead.

Ghost adventures

So, what are we to make of reports of modern-day hauntings?

First, understand that ghosts — the spirits of the departed — do not roam unseen among us; they are with the Lord in heaven or apart from Him in *Hades*.

Second, avoid fascination with modern-day "ghost adventures." At best, they rob you of your time; at worst, they draw you into demonic deception. While Satan has no power to raise the dead or create human flesh, he and his demons play on the field of superstition.

Third, stay armed. Paul exhorts us to put on the full armor of God so we can evade Satan's fiery darts (Eph. 6:11ff).

Finally, measure all experiences by the Scriptures, "which are able to give you wisdom for salvation through faith in Christ Jesus" (2 Tim. 3:15).

Who you gonna call? The Word of God is the ultimate Ghostbuster.

Think

Questions for personal or group study

What are the dangers for a Christian pursuing paranormal experience?

Suppose your friend tells you her deceased mother visited her in the night. What biblically faithful explanations might you offer?

Why do you think the Bible prohibits us from seeking communication with the deceased?

Why doesn't God permit Satan to resurrect the dead? The Lord seems to give the Devil considerable latitude in other areas, doesn't He (see 1 Peter 5:8)?

Read 2 Cor. 11:14-15. How does this passage provide an explanation for some of today's ghost stories?

Share

Talking points for discussing ghosts and the unseen realm

- Despite alleged "proof" that spirits of the dead are all around us and want to make their presence known, Christians must gauge all truth claims by the Bible, the ultimate and unchanging measure of reality.

- Scripture teaches that all humans possess both physical and non-physical properties — the body and the soul/spirit, the second of which survives physical death.

- Nowhere does the Bible support the notion that spirits of the dead (*phantasma* or *pneuma* in the Greek) are free to return to the physical realm prior to their future resurrection.

- The souls of the dead either are in the presence of God in heaven or separated from Him in torment in *Hades*.

- In Scripture, appearances of the righteous dead on earth (for example, Samuel, Moses, and Elijah) are brief and rare exceptions to the rule.

- We should avoid fascination with modern-day "ghost adventures." At best, they rob us of our time; at worst, they draw us into demonic deception. While Satan has no power to raise the dead or create human flesh, he and his demons play on the field of superstition.

twelve
How the World Ends

Remember December 21, 2012? If you believed doomsayers or John Cusack movies, the world was supposed to end that day. That was the date of the so-called Mayan Apocalypse, when an important cycle of the Maya Long Count Calendar drew to a close.

The date came and went, and we're still here. So much for end-of-days predictions that have made and broken pundits and self-proclaimed prophets for millennia. Not to be outdone by religious fanaticism, contemporary culture embraces the drama of a cataclysmic end to the world.

For example, in the 1979 film *Mad Max*, a shortage of fossil fuels drives the breakdown of society, prompting leather-clad motorcyclists to terrorize anyone with a full tank of gas.

In *Planet of the Apes*, astronaut George Taylor discovers he has traveled through space and time, returning to an earth where humans are mute and loud-mouthed armor-wearing apes are in charge.

In Ray Bradbury's frightening short story, *August 2026: There Will Come Soft Rains*, a robotic house continues to serve its human tenants long after they have become burnt silhouettes on the wall, presumably the victims of a nuclear holocaust.

And in *Hitchhiker's Guide to the Galaxy*, Arthur Dent wakes up to learn his home has been slated for demolition to make room for a new bypass; worse, the planet is set for destruction because officials from Earth never made it to Alpha Centauri to protest the demolition orders.

Whether frightening or funny, the end of the world is a topic of considerable interest and much debate. World religions and cults often contrive detailed apocalyptic views, including specific dates that, when missed, leave their leaders disgraced and their followers asking neighbors to return the cookware they thought they would never need again.

Seven biblical truths

In truth, Christians know that this sinful and fallen world — that is, the world order alienated from God, in rebellion against Him, and under the rule of Satan — will pass away. The Bible tells us so. And while evangelical Christians may debate the order of events yet to unfold, we can all agree on seven biblical truths about how the world will end.

First, the world will end when the Father says so. Jesus makes this clear in His narratives and parables. He tells His followers,

"Now concerning that day and hour no one knows — neither the angels in heaven, nor the Son — except the Father only" (Matt. 24:36). The first-century Jew hearing the parable of the 10 virgins understands that no wedding begins until the father declares everything is ready. Meanwhile, Jesus cautions us to "be alert, because you don't know either the day or the hour" (Matt. 25:13).

Second, the world will end with the return of Jesus. It's important that we look for His physical and visible return. An unseen appearance in 1914, as Jehovah's Witnesses teach,[1] strips Jesus of His physical resurrection and thus His finished work of redemption. Remember what the angels tell the disciples as they witness Jesus' ascension: "This Jesus, who has been taken from you into heaven, will come in the same way that you have seen Him going into heaven" (Acts 1:11).

Third, the world will end with the resurrection of the dead. Christians are divided as to whether all people are resurrected at the same time, or whether there are multiple resurrections stretching across 1,000 years or more. But let's not allow our interpretations to get in the way of Jesus' plain teaching that "a time is coming when all who are in the graves will hear His voice and come out" (John 5:28-29).

Fourth, the world will end with the final judgment of all people. Believers will appear before the judgment seat of Christ and be rewarded for our faithfulness (2 Cor. 5:10). Unbelievers will stand before the great white throne and be punished for their works against the kingdom of God (Rev. 20:11-15).

Fifth, the world will end with a separation of God's people from those who have rejected Him. Jesus promises His followers, "I will come back and receive you to Myself, so that where I am you may be also" (John 14:3). Unbelievers, however, are cast into hell, which Jesus describes as "outer darkness," a terrifying depiction of eternity far away from the Light of the world.

Sixth, the world will end with the creation of new heavens and a new earth. Peter gives us the image of a fiery purging in which our sinful and fallen world is refined into new heavens and a new earth (2 Peter 3:10-13). Revelation 21-22 provides further details of a restored creation.

Seventh, the world will end as human history began — with God dwelling with us. The restored earth will be our home and His throne. John hears a loud voice from God's throne declaring, "Look! God's dwelling is with humanity, and He will live with them. They will be His people, and God Himself will be with them and be their God" (Rev. 21:3).

So, don't sweat the Hollywood hype or fanatical predictions. The end of the world, and its new beginning, are in the hands of its sovereign Creator.

Think

Why do you think so many people share a strange fascination with end-of-the-world predictions?

For something as important as the return of Christ, why isn't the Bible more specific about the exact order of events?

Christians have eagerly awaited the return of Jesus for nearly 2,000 years. How might we respond to those who say we're waiting in vain — that He's not coming back?

How do we know Jesus hasn't already returned invisibly, as Jehovah's Witnesses claim?

In what ways will the return of Jesus set things right?

Share

Talking points for discussing the end of the world

- Religious fanatics and cultural icons often promote cataclysmic predictions of the end of the world. But the Bible is clear that the end of days is in the hands of our sovereign God.

- Evangelical Christians may debate the order of events yet to unfold, but we can agree on clear biblical teachings about how the world will end.

- Jesus said only the Father knows the day and hour of Christ's return; our task is not to predict, but to prepare.

- Several events are to unfold surrounding the return of Christ, including the resurrection and final judgment of all people, a separation of the righteous from the wicked, and the creation of new heavens and a new earth.

- The world will end as human history began — with God dwelling with us.

thirteen

Where Are You Spending Eternity?

Now that we've seen what God has revealed in His Word about the afterlife, a larger-than-life personal question looms: Where are *you* spending eternity? The answer may be found in your response to the question Jesus asks in Matt. 16:15 — "Who do you say that I am?"

Jesus' disciples are aware of many opinions about Him. Some have declared Jesus to be John the Baptist; others, Elijah, Jeremiah, or another prophet. But Simon Peter offers the correct answer to Jesus' question: "You are the Messiah [Christ], the Son of the living God!" (Matt. 16:16). It isn't good enough to have a high view of Jesus. To obtain everlasting life in the presence of God, we must have the correct view.

So, what does Peter's answer really mean for you, personally? How does declaring Jesus as the Messiah, the Son of the living God, determine your destiny? Consider the gravity of Peter's response.

Four considerations

First, declaring Jesus the Son of God means acknowledging that He holds your destiny in His hands. As the eternal Son of God, Jesus is the Creator, Sustainer, and the Savior of all (Luke 2:11; John 1:1-3; Phil. 2:5-11; Col. 1:15-17; 1 John 4:14). He loves you and wants to have a personal relationship with you. Understanding that Jesus is the sovereign Lord of the universe is a vital first step.

Second, declaring Jesus the Son of God means admitting there is a problem, and that problem is sin. All people are sinners, and all of us fall short of God's standard of perfection. Our sin separates us from God and invites His righteous wrath (Rom. 3:10, 23; 6:23). Left to our own devices, we would persist in a life in rebellion against our Creator, and pass into eternity apart from Him forever. Thankfully, God didn't leave us to wallow hopelessly in sin (Luke 19:10).

Third, declaring Jesus the Son of God means confessing that He is God's solution to your sin problem. Jesus left the glory of heaven and came to earth to rescue you. Even though, in His earthly existence, He was tempted in every way you are, He lived a sinless life. That way, He could stand in your place and receive the penalty meant for you (2 Cor. 5:21; Heb. 4:15-16). He died on the cross and was buried to take away your sins, and He rose physically from the dead on the third day to defeat Satan, sin, and death for you (1 Cor. 15:3-4).

Fourth, declaring Jesus the Son of God means receiving forgiveness of sins and everlasting life from Jesus as a gift. He has done all the work necessary, and He freely offers all people life with Him. In fact, Jesus lays out the requirements for everlasting life in these words: "Anyone who *hears* My word and *believes* Him who sent Me has eternal life and will not come under judgment but has passed from death to life" (John 5:24, emphasis added).

In other words, if you hear the good news about Jesus and believe in Him, you have everlasting life — right now. Sounds simple, doesn't it? But resist the temptation to add to Jesus' finished work on the cross. You may feel you have to do *something* to earn God's favor. You don't. Jesus did it for you.

The benefits of saying yes

When you say yes to Jesus, many wonderful things happen. To name just a few:

- The Holy Spirit has made you spiritually alive; you've been *born again* or *regenerated* (John 3:3-8; Eph. 2:1; Col. 2:13; Titus 3:5; 1 Peter 1:3, 23).

- You are forgiven of your sins and declared in right standing with God; that is, you are *justified* (Rom. 4:4-5; Gal. 2:16), and God will never again hold your sins against you (Ps. 103:12; Isa. 43:25; Acts 3:19; Col. 1:13-14; Heb. 10:17).

- The Holy Spirit takes up permanent residence in your heart. You are *indwelled* by the Spirit; *baptized*, or placed spiritually, into the church, known as the Body of Christ; and *sealed*, or marked out as belonging forever to the Lord Jesus (1 Cor. 3:16; 1 Cor. 12:13; Eph. 4:30).

- You are *sanctified*, or set apart as belonging to God, and the indwelling Holy Spirit helps you become more like Jesus (1 Cor. 6:11; 2 Cor. 5:17; Gal. 2:20; Phil. 1:6; 1 Thess. 5:23).

- You are an *adopted* child of God (John 1:12; Gal. 4:5-7; Eph. 1:5).

- Your name is written in the Lamb's book of life (Luke 10:20; Rev. 3:5).

- Rejoicing breaks out in heaven (Luke 15:10).

- Christ prepares a home in heaven for you, and He promises to take you there one day (John 14:1-3).

All this — an everlasting, unbreakable relationship with Jesus — is yours. Not because you're a good person. Not because you joined the right religious organization. Not because you slavishly followed a rigid set of rules in the hopes of earning God's favor. But because God has graciously offered you everlasting life as a gift — purchased through the death, burial, and resurrection of His Son.

You're going to spend eternity someplace, but you don't have to wait for death to discover where. Everlasting life is real. And it begins, not after you die, but the moment you trust in Jesus. Would you consider praying something like this:

Dear God: I have come to realize that You love me. You created me, and You invite me into an everlasting relationship with You. But I am a sinner, and my rebellion against You separates me from You. I deserve Your righteous wrath. Thankfully, You didn't abandon me in my sin. You sent Your Son, Jesus Christ, to die on the cross to pay the penalty for my sins, and to rise from the dead to give me victory over the grave. I believe this, and I place my life in Your hands. I turn from my rebellion — my unbelief and my sinful ways — and turn to You. Thank You for the gift of everlasting life. From this moment forward, I belong to You. Helped by the Holy Spirit, I will seek daily to grow more faithful and spiritually mature, until that day I draw my last breath and see You face to face.

If you prayed to receive Christ, tell someone. Jesus says, "Therefore, everyone who will acknowledge Me before men, I will also acknowledge him before My Father in heaven" (Matt. 10:32). Find a local Bible-teaching church where you can take your first step of obedience in believer's baptism, and start growing in your relationship with the Lord as you worship with others who know Jesus. Go online to mobaptist.org/church-finder to find a Missouri Baptist church near you. Or, if you live outside Missouri, visit sbc.net/churchsearch.

Think

Questions for personal or group study

Why is the answer to Jesus' question, "Who do you say that I am?" so important?

What are you acknowledging when you say that Jesus is the Messiah (or Christ), the Son of the living God?

Why do you think some people have a hard time accepting Jesus' offer of everlasting life?

Is it possible for a good, moral, church-going, upstanding citizen to spend eternity apart from Christ? Why or why not?

What are the requirements Jesus lays down for everlasting life in John 5:24?

What are the benefits of saying yes to Jesus? Which of these benefits take place in your heart, and which occur in heaven?

How important do you think it is for a new believer in Jesus to find a local church? Why?

Share

Talking points for discussing where you spend eternity

- The answer to the question, "Where are you spending eternity?" is found in your response to the words of Jesus in Matt. 16:15 — "Who do you say that I am?"

- Declaring Jesus the Son of God means, first of all, acknowledging that He holds your destiny in His hands. He loves you and wants to have a personal relationship with you.

- Second, declaring Jesus the Son of God means admitting there is a problem, and that problem is sin. Our sin separates us from God and invites His righteous wrath.

- Third, declaring Jesus the Son of God means confessing that He is God's solution to your sin problem. Jesus left the glory of heaven and came to earth to rescue you.

- Lastly, declaring Jesus the Son of God means receiving forgiveness of sins and everlasting life from Jesus as a gift. He has done all the work necessary, and He freely offers you life with Him.

- All this — an everlasting, unbreakable relationship with Jesus — is yours. Not because you're a good person. But because God has graciously offered you everlasting life as a gift — purchased through the death, burial, and resurrection of His Son.

Notes

Chapter 1: Ten Biblical Truths About the Afterlife

1. Todd Burpo, found at http://www.oneplace.com/ministries/ask-hank/download-buy/books/life-after-life-after-life.html, accessed Oct. 12, 2015.

2. *Heaven is for Real: A Little Boy's Astounding Story of His Trip to Heaven and Back* by Colton Burpo and Lynn Vincent (Nashville, TN: Thomas Nelson, 2010).

3. *To Hell and Back: Life After Death – Startling New Evidence* by Maurice S. Rollins (Nashville, TN: Thomas Nelson, 1993).

4. Hank Hanegraaff, found at http://www.oneplace.com/ministries/ask-hank/download-buy/books/life-after-life-after-life.html.

5. C.S. Lewis, *The Problem of Pain* (Kindle Edition, HarperCollins e-books, 2009).

Chapter 2: Sheol and the Afterlife

1. Robert A. Morey, *Death and the Afterlife* (Minneapolis, MN: Bethany House Publishers, 1984), 74-75.

Chapter 3: Hades and the Afterlife

n/a

Chapter 4: Does the Bible Teach Purgatory?

1. *Catechism of the Catholic Church* (New York: Doubleday, 1995), 291.

2. John A. Hardon, *Pocket Catholic Dictionary* (New York: Image Books, 1985), 93.

3. *The Apologetics Study Bible* (Nashville, TN: Holman Bible Publishers, 2007), 1541.

4. Harry Blamires, *Knowing the Truth About Heaven & Hell: Our Choices and Where They Lead Us* (Ann Arbor, MI: Servant Books, 1988), 85.

5. Joseph Loconte, "When Luther Shook Up Christianity," *Wall St. Journal*, Oct. 30, 2015, A11.

6. *Catechism of the Catholic Church*, 295.

Chapter 5: Your Future Resurrection

1. *Expository Dictionary of Bible Words: Word Studies for Key English Bible Words Based on the Hebrew and Greek Texts*, Stephen D. Renn, ed. (Peabody, MA: Hendrickson Publishers, 2005), 388.

2. *The Book of Revelation: A Commentary on the Greek Text*, NIGTC (Grand Rapids, MI: Eerdmans, 1999), 191; quoted in *The New American Commentary: An Exegetical and Theological Exposition of Holy Scripture, Vol. 39: Revelation* (Nashville, TN: B&H Publishing Group, 2012), 60.

3. The fact that Jesus retains the marks of His crucifixion in His glorified body does not mean that you and I keep our scars, deformities, and disfigurations after our resurrection. Our physical imperfections result *from* sin; Christ's wounds are borne *for* our sins. Further, His marks are everlasting evidence of His redemptive work on our behalf, and helps us positively identify Him in the company of false Messiahs.

Chapter 6: Everyone's Day of Reckoning

1. *Dictionary of Biblical Prophecy and End Times* (Grand Rapids, MI: Zondervan, 2007), 236.

2. *The Apocalypse: An Exposition of the Book of Revelation* (Grand Rapids, MI: Kregel Publications, 1900), 479.

3. *Ibid.*, 479.

4. *Insights on Revelation* (Grand Rapids, MI: Zondervan, 2011), 266-67.

Chapter 7: Gehenna and the Afterlife

1. Everlasting "separation" from God in hell does not undermine God's omnipresence, since it is meant in terms of relationship, intimacy, or fellowship. Scripture teaches that those who worship

the beast are tormented forever with fire and sulfur "in the sight of the holy angels and in the sight of the Lamb" (see Rev. 14:9-11).

2. Steve Gregg, *All You Want to Know About Hell: Three Christian Views of God's Final Solution to the Problem of Sin* (Nashville, TN: Thomas Nelson, 2013), 86-98.

3. Robert A. Morey, *Death and the Afterlife* (Minneapolis, MN: Bethany House Publishers, 1984), 90.

Chapter 8: The Goodness of Hell

1. Dinesh D'Souza, *Godforsaken: Bad Things Happen. Is there a God who cares? Yes. Here's proof* (U.S.A.: Tyndale House Publishers, Inc., Reprint edition 2012), 224.

2. Robert Ingersoll, cited in Martin Gardner, *The Whys of a Philosophical Scrivener* (New York: St. Martin's Press, 1999), 301.

3. John Stott, cited in D'Souza, *Godforsaken*, 226.

4. C.S. Lewis, *The Problem of Pain*, cited in "Banished from Humanity: C.S. Lewis and the Doctrine of Hell" by Randy Alcorn, March 18, 2015, http://www.desiringgod.org/articles/banished-from-humanity.

5. Lewis, *The Problem of Pain*, cited in "Seeing Hell through the Reason and Imagination of C.S. Lewis" by Douglas Beyer, Jan. 1, 1998, http://www.discovery.org/a/507.

Chapter 9: Is Heaven Our Final Home?

1. Randy Alcorn, *Heaven* (Wheaton, IL: Tyndale House Publishers, 2004), 42.

2. *Theological Dictionary of the New Testament*, Gerhard Kittel and Gerhard Friedrich, editors (Grand Rapids, MI: William B. Eerdmans Publishing Company, 1985), 388.

3. J.I. Packer, quoted in Hank Hanegraaff, *AfterLife: What You Need to Know About Heaven, the Hereafter & Near-death Experiences* (Brentwood, TN: Worthy Publishing, 2013), 16.

Chapter 10: A Look into Tartarus

1. *The Apologetics Study Bible* (Nashville, TN: Holman Bible Publishers, 2007), 1859.

Chapter 11: Should You Believe in Ghosts?

1. Hank Hanegraaff, *Afterlife: What You Need to Know about Heaven, the Hereafter & Near-death Experiences* (Brentwood, TN: Worthy Publishing, 2013), 115.

Chapter 12: How the World Will End

1. *The Greatest Man Who Ever Lived* (New York: Watch Tower Bible & Tract Society, 1991), 132.

Chapter 13: Where Are You Spending Eternity?

n/a

Additional Resources

Other apologetics resources available from the MBC:

The Last Apologist: A Commentary on Jude for Defenders of the Christian Faith

The Apologist's Tool Kit: Resources to Help You Defend the Christian Faith

What Every Christian Should Know about Islam: A Primer on the Muslim Faith from a Biblical Perspective

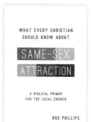

What Every Christian Should Know about Same-sex Attraction: A Biblical Primer for the Local Church

Order printed copies at **mobaptist.org/apologetics**

Print and Kindle editions available from Amazon